MC MONEY MORE FUN

SHARE YOUR KNOW-HOW IN AN ONLINE COURSE AND ENJOY THE RECURRING INCOME

LORRAINE GANNON

www.get-known.co.uk

DEDICATION

To my husband Rick and my children Ben and Charlotte, I dedicate this book. You are my reason why and I love you with all my heart. Here's to having many more years of fun together!

CONTENTS

CHAPTER 12
EXPRESSIONS OF INTEREST

CHAPTER 13
EXECUTE

CHAPTER 14
ENGAGE

INTRODUCTION

"If you don't find a way to make money while

you sleep, you will work until you die."

WARREN BUFFETT

HOW MUCH FUN ARE YOU HAVING?

Some entrepreneurs have all the fun. They only spend their time on things they want to do, and they only work on projects and with people that interest them. Because of this, they actually love what they do, it shows and is written all over their face. They are vibrant and full of energy. They actually have time to read and learn about new developments and they effortlessly implement new ideas into their successful, ever-evolving businesses.

That's not all. They also earn more money. This means that not only can they go on fancy family holidays and really enjoy life, they also have money to test and measure new strategies in their businesses. Having built successful businesses, they share their knowledge and train others to do what they do. They abundantly share their secrets. They are not scared to give away their best content. They are generous, inspiring and happy. They are in control of their lives, and loving it.

However, the majority of entrepreneurs are not having that kind of fun or making that kind of money. They work all hours God sends, are at their clients' constant beck and call and panic at the beginning of every month when their cash flow starts at zero. They don't even realise they are burning themselves out to hustle and grind their way to success. They are exhausted by the stresses of running a business and can't remember what a work-life balance is.

So what's the secret, and how can you be more like the guys having more fun and making more money? How can you get from wherever you are with your business today, however burnt out you may feel from all the blood, sweat and tears you have poured into your business, to being one of those entre-preneurs who is having a great time and has the power to choose how to spend their time both in and outside of work?

In this book, I'm going to show you how you can have more money and more fun, no matter where you are with your business today. I'm going to show you how to create an online course that will bring your business reliable recurring income. You will no longer need to kill yourself in the 9-5. You will rekindle some of the energy you had at the beginning of your business journey and have more choice in the work you decide to take on.

IS YOUR BUSINESS GIVING YOU THE FREEDOM YOU THOUGHT IT WOULD?

When I left my corporate job, I was the most miserable I have ever been in my life. I had a salary. I had to fill in a timesheet every week to ensure I was meeting my contracted hours. I took a brave step into self-employment and started my own consultancy company. I thought this would give me the finan-cial freedom, time and fun I craved. However, I found I was still delivering a time-valued outcome for clients (basically I sold them my time) and although this gave me more money, it did not give me any more time or fun. I remember the stress, when I was on holiday dealing with a client's issues on my hotel room balcony. I soon felt chained to my business and burnt out by my clients, who I was now beholden to regardless of what my agenda was. It was unsustainable and something a lot of us struggle with.

So many people who start businesses find themselves at this point. Maybe you can relate? Stress is cumulative and it can be one small thing that tips you over the edge. Entrepreneurs are particularly susceptible to burnout because we take so much on, push ourselves so hard, and are always promising ourselves we will slow down after the next big project is finished. However, we are only human and each have our limits.

I knew something had to change. I enjoyed sharing my expertise with clients, but there had to be a better way than just invoicing for my time. Slowly, I learnt to create products that had recurring income. This recurring income took the pressure off my business and meant I didn't have to work all the hours that God sent, and, as a bonus, I could pick and choose my clients so that I only took on the most interesting work. I also got to do cool things like take my children on lots of holidays (where I could actually switch off without worrying about clients calling and interrupting my family time).

HOW RECURRING INCOME CHANGED EVERYTHING

Whilst I was working for myself, my husband was in the police force where he worked shifts. I was also working long hours and this combined was killing our family life.

We already had a couple of rental properties at this point, and we decided to take property seriously so my husband could quit his job. Using very little of our own capital, our income grew and, over time, we replaced my husband's salary and my consultancy income with the recurring income streams from our property investments. Having our bills paid by recurring rental income gave us our freedom and fun back as a family. We were no longer stressed about money and could make sure we were always home when the kids came back from school. But this was just the beginning...

People naturally asked us how we achieved this, so we decided to write an online course about it in a very specific way and created another income stream out of our knowledge. This was our first online course and a total game-changer. I pushed hard for us to not sacrifice our recently reclaimed weekends to train new property investors. Having a digital asset meant people could learn whenever they wanted and it also gave us serious scalability. Even if we had given up one weekend a month, we'd only have reached a classroom's worth of people at a time; with an online course, it's limitless.

The course structure, the marketing and the delivery were unique, and because of the way it was designed, the course went on to earn us £20k per month. This radically changed our family's life. We could afford to go away on regular fancy family holidays, city breaks and even cruises.

Over time, I realised there was a simple formula to creating and running a successful online course and it became apparent that not everyone knew the secret, so I decided to teach other entrepreneurs stuck in the time for money trap like I was how to get out! Over the last four years I've helped people build courses in a range of sectors and honed my methodology.

This book has been written based on the learnings and marketing skills I picked up in the field. These skills have been tried and tested both on my own products and other people's products. There is a reason why my easy, 3-step methodology is set out in the way it is, and with the key steps in order.

There is no point skipping to any part of the book because without one part then the whole does not make sense. The methodology is designed to give you early success. Early success is often seen as a good indicator of long-term continued results. Quick wins are long-term wins too. You create momentum the quicker you can find some early successes. The methodology in this book is deliberately set out to help you get income quickly, so you can relax early on and develop your course to avoid burnout.

READY FOR MORE MONEY AND MORE FUN?

The title *More Money, More Fun* is deliberately focused on the outcome I want for you. Fun is a factor of freedom, time and money. You might have jobs and clients that you hate and would love to get rid of. I am giving you a way to avoid those jobs and clients and to make choices about what you want to do with your time and freedom. Relying on revenues from work you hate and don't enjoy is not a good long-term plan and can lead to financial self-sabotage and a poor state of self-satisfaction, along with burnout, depression and a host of other things you don't want to invite in.

READY TO MAKE BETTER USE OF YOUR TIME?

I love what I do, I love learning and I love the gift of time that is life. It has taken me years to realise this. When I train mentees to work towards financial freedom, I always ask them why they want it. Everyone gives the same answer: freedom. We all want freedom to choose what to do and how to spend our time, yet few of us are really in control of this.

We each have two valuable finite resources: our time and our self. The reality is, the only true resource we have is time. We have 86,400 seconds each day. Each day we wake up is a gift of time we have been given. I have come to realise how short life is. Now is a unique moment in time to start this project for yourself. You have probably picked this book up at the perfect point in your life, never will you have developed your ideas, passion and knowledge to the point you have now. Yet there will be no point in delaying, the market will help you decide if your knowledge is worth something.

However, I believe that we are all conditioned to forget about how short our lives are. We put it out of our minds and only think about today and tomorrow. Looking for short-term gratification and results drives us to find quick wins and avoid some of the tougher decisions and hard work. This is just human psychology; we are all guilty of it. But I want you to take a second to appreciate that you don't have forever, and the perfect time to make a positive change to reclaim your freedom is now.

Ready to make a change? Let's get started.

MY STORY –
ROCK BOTTOM

"You build on failure. You use it as a stepping stone. Close the door on the past. You don't try to forget the mistakes, but you don't dwell on it. You don't let it have any of your energy, or any of your time, or any of your space."

JOHNNY CASH

PERSPECTIVE AND TIME

Perspective is a powerful tool. I believe that accepting other people's perspectives is one of the reasons the world has so many challenges today. If we all had the same view and experiences, we would be able to understand the reasons why we all do the things we do. There would be more harmony and agreement. However, we can't control all of the variables in the world, and despite us trying our best to negotiate and push for our dreams, it doesn't always happen.

Your perspective changes too. Have you ever heard a song when you're in a bad mood and you hate it, then you hear it when you're at a party and you love it? I know people that have changed their whole life plans in 12 months because they have had a change in perspective.

We all want to enjoy our time and do really positive things, but sometimes life can knock the stuffing out of us. It can bring us down for weeks and months. Some dreams and goals are harder than others to achieve. Without reason, your time and opportunity can run out. Something really crap can happen, just as it was all just going to plan.

Until I was 28 years old, there wasn't much about my life that I really wanted to change. I would have liked a bigger house, more money to go on holiday, perhaps a nicer car, and the top finance job in the company where I was working (although this seemed a little more hassle than I wanted) but nothing particularly that I felt I needed to change.

2004

In May 2004, while six months pregnant with my son, I experienced serious complications. To this day, I still sometimes feel guilty that I did something wrong. To be honest, sharing these few vulnerable sentences has held me back, and I have had to forgive myself and coach myself that I have the courage to forgive myself, if I have anything to forgive.

I had the tiniest baby in May 2004, my son, Ben. He weighed only 3lb 15 ounces. He was born 10 weeks early after an emergency caesarean section and other complications. To me, he was perfect. Seven months earlier I had thought that starting my family would be just another fun thing in my life, that everything would carry on, and that I would embrace the role of modern career mum and manage to juggle all parts of my life perfectly.

THE WORST NEWS

Then, in October 2004 when Ben was only a few months old, I was told he would struggle to walk, that his life would be a struggle, that he would need lots of help to achieve his best in life. I was told Ben had Cerebral palsy or brain damage. Months and months of having a screaming baby had worn me down. I heard the words and I had nothing to say. I picked up my coat, put Ben in his pushchair and walked straight out of the hospital.

The reality I had to accept was that our son was born 10 weeks early and I had an infection that resulted in him getting brain damage. We didn't find out until Ben was a few months old. I didn't see it coming, even though Ben had been crying for the first four months of his life.

On finding out Ben had brain damage, my heart cracked and ached in my chest and I couldn't talk about it for weeks. I just cried. It took years to recover from the grief and to get to grips with the impact. You hear of miracles of people recovering, but if something is broken, it is broken, it cannot be mended, it cannot be returned to perfect, there is always that consistent broken part.

EVERYTHING CHANGED

Before Ben was born, I had a corporate career as an accountant in a large business, I worked until 7 most evenings and received a pretty ordinary salary. After Ben was born, nothing was the same. I couldn't manage a career and look after Ben. My husband worked shifts in the police force, and we both realised we needed to do something different with our lives.

We turned our lives upside down and bought a gastro pub and ran that together as a family. It was the worst business idea because we were always busy at family times. Evenings and weekends were taken up running a busy pub. Over the next few years, we worked hard and we realised we made more money out of buying and selling property in pubs than running a business of pubs. So we bought a few more pubs in our area hoping to trade them up and sell them. However, it was tough – we had five pubs all with high-volume service-led transactions. The profit margins were slim and competitive. We sold our pubs when a big pub company gave us a silly

"

I realised that there would be a time where I wouldn't be able to cope with the challenges of looking after a disabled child, my daughter, maintaining a career and, importantly, having some work-life balance and fun. It all was so boring and unfulfilling.

"

amount of money for a pub. We realised that the pub business was hard work and completely unfriendly for family life.

Once we sold the pubs, it was then time to decide what to do next. I took a temporary role as an accountant again in 2008 for a few years. It was a challenge because I was pregnant again with my daughter, Charlotte. I was very miserable in my role. My boss made me feel inadequate. There was always toxic office politics going on and I decided I couldn't keep on this treadmill, exchanging my time for money. It was not what I wanted. I have always been looking for growth and am naturally very entrepreneurial.

I realised that there would be a time where I wouldn't be able to cope with the challenges of looking after a disabled child, my daughter, maintaining a career and, importantly, having some work-life balance and fun. It all was so boring and unfulfilling.

I gradually took a few tentative steps to explore what I could do. I trained as an accountant, so I thought perhaps I could start a tax and bookkeeping business. However, I soon realised that I didn't want the responsibility of managing 300 clients' tax returns, the demands and the pressure of keeping on top of that workload was too much. Having been in business before, and because I understood the pressure of cash flow, I knew I didn't want a service-led business. I was looking for a good business model. I turned to franchising to see what might be available.

I thought if I could buy into a good model where others had already had success then it would be a great way to copy something that already worked. There is nothing wrong with copying a good model. The trick is to find a good model to copy and not copy the flawed model. I researched lots of franchise models that I felt would give me the right outcome. I became a franchised partner of a procurement business.

I chose a business in consultancy that focused on procurement and how I could help businesses to make more profit. There was a recurring income model in so far as if my clients got savings, I got a percentage for a fixed period.

However, over time, my initial energy for my business started to drop, and it became exhausting to keep delivering at the standards needed to reach a decent income.

My cash flow had initially grown quite quickly, and I was hoping for a way to scale. However, I soon realised that my results were all completely reliant on my own efforts and energy. I had to deliver for my clients, they expected to see me, and they wanted results. I was driving up and down the motorways, sometimes travelling for six hours a day to clients who were only trying to reduce my fees or get out of contracts. I had no residual income that propped up the bigger clients and projects. If I was at all distracted away from my business, my income took a drop.

And I had been distracted. I had learnt how to invest in high cash flow property. I had been distracted by property and when our property income started to grow significantly through Houses in Multiple Occupation H.M.O.'s (house shares or multi-lets), which we started investing in 2012.

My consultancy business started to suffer but, having been quite successful at growing our own portfolio, I started to train others in property investment online. It was very deliberate. The outcome was to avoid selling my time or my husband's to train people ongoing. We had a young family; we needed our weekends for quality family time together.

This is when we looked at how we could achieve an outcome that could scale. A profitable product that didn't need me or my husband to do all the heavy lifting. We also looked at how the products of the business could be systemised and automated yet delivered with huge value to the customer.

Starting with the end in mind, I recognised that we needed a product that had a lifespan. I read some books about the membership economy and also reflected that I had direct debits for gyms, clubs and other subscriptions that I took out and never got around to cancelling because one day I might use the product. The products were always low-level pricing but that meant I didn't leave as a customer. We needed to keep customers for as long as possible and to have the content and course systematically delivered to them. It worked brilliantly. It has completely transformed our lives.

WHY BEING IN THE WORST PLACE IN LIFE IS THE BEST PLACE TO START

Hitting rock bottom forced us to think our lives through and work out what it was we really wanted. Had Ben not been born with such challenges it might have been quite easy for me to find a job that I could have managed in some sort of fashion.

I would encourage you to use your situation as a catalyst for change. Identify the outcome you are looking for and go find it.

There is a little bit of magic and amazing in the rock bottom of your life. What's yours?

Shit happens. How you deal with it defines your life. I have had career lows, business lows and personal lows. Each situation has brought with it new learnings and new opportunities. However, I know the feeling of helplessness, and being out of control kills your motivation, and a feeling of 'Why bother?' hangs around like a dark cloud. Daily life continues, you just carry on, but all tasks become chores.

I don't know what has happened in your life, but chances are that you are reading this book because you want something significant to change. I also train others in how to use property strategies and I've noticed a lot of success stories are born out of a challenge. Any problem or life change that affects your health or family's happiness can be the motivator behind making massive changes in your life. It seems human beings are more motivated to move away from pain than move

"

I would encourage you to use your situation as a catalyst for change. Identify the outcome you are looking for and go find it.

"

towards rewards, often the carrot is not enough on its own. We need to feel the pain and the impact of something before we are motivated to move towards the solution.

I have seen some of our course students succeed on a huge scale when the 'worst' happens to them. They lose their jobs, or their clients stop paying them. It is sometimes the shock they need to change their lives. The fact that all of a sudden, they have to find new ways of finding enough income each month that really transforms their thinking. I've seen people go on to build property portfolios, build training programmes and develop their businesses because they had to.

Make it your starting point of success.

The trouble with being fairly comfortable with your situation, is you are not out of your comfort zone, you are happily settling for the circumstances you find yourself in.

Comfort zones are dangerous in that they can gradually change over time and without a sudden moment of pain or discomfort, most people become miserable and sit around in their comfortable spaces and eventually become disenchanted with the world. Think of this rather cruel but interesting analogy: a frog that is put into a pot of boiling water jumps straight out and survives, whereas a frog that is put in a cold pot of water that is slowly heated till it boils stays in the pot and dies. The frog gets used to its surroundings and doesn't move, and he dies.

Hitting rock bottom is powerful for you because you know you can cope and you know you have survived the worst, there's not much left that could challenge you. Over time you can look back and see that low point as the start of changes in your life. It makes you move. Eventually, you become some-what grateful to your rock bottom, you realise it has been part of the journey. How can you know success without failure? How can you know hot without cold and happiness without sadness? It's the best and worst thing that has ever happened to you!

PART ONE

WHY DO WE GET UP EVERY DAY AND WORK TILL WE DIE?

PART ONE

When we start businesses, we think they are the answer to all our lifestyle and financial problems. Goodbye stress, timesheets and bad managers; hello financial freedom. But if we're not careful, we can wake up a few years later and realise we jumped out of the frying pan and into the fire. In Part One I'm going to show you how the time for money trap works and show you exactly how you can take control of getting yourself out of it.

The time for money trap can creep up without you realising. It is effectively where you trade your time (to an employer or client) for money. Think about it: when you start a job or career, you progress and can often get pay rises and promotions. You buy a new house, a new car, holidays and start living to the level of pay you receive. Then, when you realise you have to pay for all these things, you look around and notice you *need* the income and therefore are trapped in the job just to stay afloat. A jump out of the role would mean either joining a competitor or changing industries or specialism. Starting up a new business would mean a drop in income and often a cash flow roller-coaster for a few years. So you stay in that job that you never particularly wanted and don't particularly enjoy and keep selling your time, every day, to your employer.

I left corporate because I felt undervalued and I had no control over my personal happiness. It was no fun. I was often stuck in the middle of a political agenda. I was just a pawn in a chess game, being told to move from one position to another.

I saw people crack under the pressure of appraisals and performance reviews, challenged to over deliver and rise above expectations in return for poor rewards and platitudes. No one once tried to help me make more money in my job or make it more fun. It was always about how much could they get out of me for as little pay as possible.

Everyone was jostling for the position of top performer, not realising how destructive and crucifying the stress involved in getting there would be. Jobs well done were often overlooked because you chatted to your colleagues more than you should. Projects that were delivered in stressful situations, and when the team were working to 11pm, resulted in overtime being cut back because that was the nature of the department. High stress and high hours. Zero fun.

I often work with entrepreneurs and business owners that are incredibly knowledgeable but worn down by the grind of managing their staff, clients, cash flow, etc. They have worked hard for a long time, no doubt at a cost to their personal and family life. But the problem is they've swapped the corporate grind for their own grind without even realising. Then one day they sit back and perhaps don't feel well, their energy is low today and they ask themselves a pertinent question, such as:

"Who does all this work, if it's not me?"

"How do I sell or exit a business that is just me?"

"How can I possibly retire or get a better work/life balance?"

They recognise they have no asset in the business. I help them free themselves from this trap and I'm going to do the same for you...

I've been there; I remember working on one consultancy project until 2 am in my home office. I had a report to finish and I had completely underestimated the amount of time it would take me to complete – I had sold a lot more of my time for the fee than I had realised. I had committed the cardinal sin: I had undersold my time. I was meeting the client the next day, and I needed to print out the report. Disaster struck, my home office printer had run out of ink. I had to drive to my office about 20 minutes from my home to get a spare ink cartridge. Then I had to get back home and print out the report. I was a self-employed consultant, the project was all my work, so I had to go get the printer cartridge because without it I wasn't going to be able to raise an invoice. This was an unhealthy level of stress. I was working too hard, too long, for too little reward.

I recognised something had to change. I started looking for income products that were based on a recurring income theme and had some leverage that didn't require my time to get paid. Initially I found property, but this experience taught me to look at how building an asset in online courses could help me achieve the same.

There is no quick fix, but you can start to move towards the outcome you want. Deliberately decide to fix this situation and get yourself out of the time for money trap. It's never too late to start.

CHAPTER 1

WHY TRADITIONAL EMPLOYMENT HOLDS YOU BACK

"Twenty years from now you will be more disappointed by the things you didn't do than by the ones you did do."

MARK TWAIN

HAVE YOU EVER WORKED FOR AN IDIOT?

I have. I regret the years of my life I put up with it too. Why did I let myself get trodden down by the bureaucracy of a leader that couldn't find a way to motivate me? Are you in a job that makes you dread Monday mornings? Do you sit in your car dreading to go inside the office building? Unfortunately, too many of us spend our days in this misery. It's far too common.

Don't put up with incompetent leaders. You don't need to go into depression or have a nervous breakdown because of a stressful job. Sack that job.

One "idiot" boss of mine actually wrote in an appraisal document that "Lorraine thinks she's better than she really is" and this was despite winning a corporate award from the CEO for "expert in delivery".

You must never let your self-worth and mindset be reliant upon anyone else's perception of you.

Perception can be dangerous; it is just their view and not reality. Some people do not have your back, and this is why I learnt that no matter how hard I worked or how well my work was received by some, there is always someone who doesn't get your value.

If you do work for an idiot, be grateful for that because it might be the kick you need to go find another more suitable job, start a business, make some investments, just don't put up with it. Don't let your boss take your energy and soul. You don't want to go home drained every day; you want to be set free. I am now very grateful I worked for an idiot. Otherwise, I might never have been desperate enough to leave my job. I have cried and screamed in anger over my old job and my boss. I have been treated appallingly. I am really mad with myself for not doing more to stop the situation.

I've had some very painful experiences exchanging my time for money. Selling my time for money made me miserable. It put additional pressure on me to perform every single minute of every day. I needed to constantly deliver whilst being completely bored by the repetition and mundane routine of repeating tasks and processes day after day.

MY PAINFUL EXPERIENCE

My earliest memory of the time for money trap came when I was a trainee accountant and I spent the first four weeks of my job in the filing cupboard, reorganising files and accountancy papers. I had to record every minute I worked on a client's files and book it to them. If I had too much unchargeable time it was frowned upon. I knew what my charge out rate was,

"

I learnt that you cannot control your salary through promotion or career advancement, nothing is secure or guaranteed. I learnt not to trust my employer's view of the world and who should have which roles.

"

and I knew what my salary was. I was earning £3.33 per hour as a trainee accountant. If a client's offices were a distance from the office, I had to travel in my own time to the client. My actual hourly rate was lower because I didn't get paid for travel hours. I soon left this role.

I learnt that even hourly paid roles don't pay you for all your hours. Some job roles and businesses just breed the time for money trap. I realised I was stuck!

Technology was supposed to liberate us from the daily grind of emails, work and admin, but somehow, with the help of tablets and smartphones, we are working more than ever before, and outside of office hours. We are giving this time for free! We are all feeling overworked, drained, and potentially burnt out.

Sometimes it's impossible to win the game. In one job, I needed to pick my children up from their nursery, but a younger employee with no children could work late at the drop of a hat. One of these younger colleagues was asked to work late on an urgent task and was then rewarded by winning staff member of the month and £300 of shopping vouchers.

I learnt that I could never become staff member of the month because I always had childcare responsibilities. I couldn't join the game.

One Friday I was told I had been successful in my application for promotion and I was promoted to Chief Accountant. I went out and celebrated. I had a great time and opened a bottle of champagne. Then, on Monday morning, I was called by my boss to say the Finance Director had been changed over the weekend and all promotions were going to be reversed. I was devastated. I had no way of increasing my salary other than going for promotion. When I got the promotion I was elated. It meant an additional £1,000 per month in my pay.

I left early on that Monday after the devastating news had been given to me and I had an emotional breakdown at a junction close to my home. A man got out of his car and was annoyed with me because I was rushing him at a junction. I wanted to get home; I wanted the security of my things around me. I screamed at him to get back in the car and leave me alone. I repeated my screams over and over. He retreated quickly, scared by my mental outburst.

I learnt that you cannot control your salary through promotion or career advancement, nothing is secure or guaranteed. I learnt not to trust my employer's view of the world and who should have which roles.

IS EMPLOYMENT HOLDING YOU BACK?

You'll never be rich working for someone else. I'm very sorry but there are very few people who earn millions working for others. I know there are directors at board level, who, with their share options, do become mega rich. Very few are employed as CEOs and with share options listed on the stock exchange. This is your wake-up call.

You will never grow into your full potential. There will always be someone else who will have a different view of what you should be doing in your job. Your ideas won't always be taken on board. Your skills will make the business more money, not you. Your systems, your processes, your code, your knowledge, your inventions and your know-how, all make money for someone else. You get paid your agreed fee. You get paid to exchange your time for money.

Choose to get paid on results, choose to trust that you can deliver value that others will pay you for. You will no longer exchange time for money. There will only be the value of you making things happen, with your systems, your processes, your code, your knowledge, your inventions and your know-how. It is you and your wisdom that gets paid.

To repeat, you will never be rich working for someone else, so if that is what you are trying to do you are going to have to step outside the comfort of your salary and benefits. I know it is scary but then you are a clever and intelligent person. You know you can make it work deep down.

You might be looking to escape your job and start your own business. If you are not in the self-employed race yet, hold tight – the world is changing, and with global connectivity there are only a select few industries that will need full-time people in the future. The world is embracing flexible working practices and more people are becoming freelancers and sub-contractors than ever before. You might find yourself with a self-employed job and clients sooner than you think.

DE-RISK YOUR LIFE AND LEAVE YOUR JOB!

If you want to de-risk your life and take back control, one of the best ways to achieve that is to leave your job. Sounds crazy, right? I just said de-risk and you probably think leaving your job is a high-risk strategy. Let me explain.

Ultimately, when you are not in control of how you spend your time or the amount of money you can pay yourself, then you are handing over trust to someone else. Trust that the business doesn't overspend each month and has enough money to pay you. Trust that the owners of the business won't make you redundant next month when their overheads become too high. Trust that the leadership team are ensuring the future of the company, bringing in sales and capacity to deliver. You are not in control of these variables.

The world is changing, and technology has increased the speed at which businesses can operate. Speed can only happen where there is less resistance and friction; when a business works smarter and faster, the business will earn more money. The more automation, the more reliable the results. Businesses have to adapt to stay relevant in the market, they have to keep up with new technology to compete. People aren't staying in job roles for anywhere near as long as they used to. Whether it's the technology or the business that is giving rise to these changes is perhaps irrelevant. It is now becoming normal for a UK worker to change employer every five years on average.

In fact, when I show you how, you will find more security from your own business and other investments, and you will suddenly realise that you are more secure than you ever were as an employee or contractor. What happens when you de-risk your life and find secure freedom? You actually find fun and happiness. Fun, because you have secured an income to cover your essentials, everything else is just fun. Fun, because you can choose how to spend your time.

"There are many ways of going forward,

but only one way of standing still."

FRANKLIN D. ROOSEVELT

There is nothing more creative than the brain that trusts its ability to find a way. If you believe you can do something, the brain will find a way. If you believe you are destined to stay in your current role and get the long service award, then guess what? That is exactly what will happen. Choose a different option by just believing there is one and life will take care of the rest.

We all have limited trips around the sun. I am aiming for at least 100 trips. You only have this moment, and this is what people refer to as mindfulness. If you are here in the moment, it is difficult to experience anything else. We can only think about one thing at a time, so always being in the present is very rewarding. Fear is normally future bound and if you are in the moment, you can be free of worry and stress.

Losing your job can feel like a disaster. If you have ever been made redundant or your biggest client has gone into liquidation, then you will know that feeling of panic that comes when you lose your main income source. There is a period of shock and grieving for the "perceived" security of the income you have just lost. It is the lack of security of knowing where the money will come from that panics you the most.

The human brain will often interpret "normal routine" things as being secure. This is the fight or flight instinct handed down to us in our DNA from thousands of years of surviving on this planet. Your brain is very wary of things that change or are new because it might be a threat and it's just a natural protection pattern. Just because you have a job and do what everyone else is doing, does not mean that continuing on this is going to be the best way of earning money for you forever. The fear of not being able to pay your bills can mean you've been working in a job you hate for decades.

THE CORPORATE LIE / THE CAREER LIE

The career lie is told over and over to millions of school children and employees. The lie that there is a well-trodden path of harmony and progression; if you get yourself a career, then everything will be fine.

"Formal education will make you a living;

self-education will make you a fortune."

JIM ROHN

Unfortunately, we all fall for the lie. Get a job, work hard, you'll be promoted, you'll earn more, and life will be great. But, of course, you'll get a home, a family perhaps, a car, a few curve balls will come your way, you might get divorced, re-marry, have more kids and you might have elderly parents to look after. You might get sick and not be able to climb the corporate ladder. Life is never as simple as work hard and play hard.

We were all taught that getting smart kids to do our homework was wrong, yet many entrepreneurs praise the idea of hiring staff smarter than you to have a competitive edge. Copying a good idea is wrong, yet it is the smartest thing you can do. Are you somebody else's competitive edge?

What nobody tells you is that life is full of opinion. You work in a role where you have been educated and trained to perform. Then you hit the real world and all of a sudden everyone has an opinion, and then you are stuck in the middle of a battle of wits and office politics. Everyone is hustling to get their opinion across to improve their position and chances of promotion. It's frustrating when the rules keep changing, when the business looks for different answers, and you're not part of that equation.

I don't think there is any way to win at this game.

CHAPTER 2

THE "TIME FOR MONEY" TRAP

"If you don't value your time, neither will others. Stop giving away your time and talents. Value what you know and start charging for it."

KIM GARST

ARE YOU IN THE "TIME FOR MONEY" TRAP?

Chances are if you are reading this book you have all the necessities in life: you live in a comfortable place and can find resources to support you. But do you know someone who is earning all the money and is not as good as you? You might already have a really good business or nine-to-five job, and you're already doing really good things. You've built up great knowledge, skills and insights and you're seeing other people who don't have any of your value taking their stuff and making a lot of money out of it.

You are stressed, cynical, broke, looking for quick wins and fed up of working for money.

If you have picked up this book to have more money and fun, then I can surmise that you are most likely to be stuck in a time for money trap. To have more fun you need more freedom from financial responsibilities and commitments of time constraints. Nobody really ever buys a second of your time, they only ever buy the outcome of what you do. If you work for a client at a charge out rate or you have a call out fee, your work might be valued in hourly chunks but unless you achieve the outcome for the client then you are unlikely to get paid.

Somewhere in your life you exchange your time for money (whether you sell your time to your boss or your clients), and you are not happy about that. You've realised that at some point in your life, you will die and that means your time is limited and is not for doing something you don't enjoy. For now, the only place you can be is here, in the moment. Why would you spend your life doing something you don't want to do?

This is the biggest common problem facing small business owners. They have created a job for themselves and they hate it; they don't make enough money to have any fun anymore.

ARE YOU OUT OF BALANCE? THE TRIANGLE OF VALUE

In life, it is impossible to constantly maintain a perfect balance, there is no perfect moment. We have to constantly adjust and move back to balance to ensure we maintain the healthy proportions. The problem is some of us spend more time out of balance than we should, and our lack of balance is not sustainable in the long term. Imagine you have a triangle of resources: money, energy, time and you. You can divide the triangle up into different slices. It is a balancing act, but you get to choose how it's made up.

▶ **Money** can be spent, and money can be earnt, somewhere there is a fair exchange. It can move from you to another person if you give that person that money in exchange for their time or goods.

▶ **Energy** exists and can only be transferred and not created. Energy moves from one type to another. There is never any loss of energy, just our ability to contain it in one form.

▶ **Time** doesn't exist, there is no future or past, only hope of the future and memories of the past, so you can give time in each moment.

▶ **You** can't go to the future or the past, you are only here now.

You are at the centre of this value exchange and you can choose how to control any one of time, energy or money. It may be good enough to get a job and sell your time. You may become self-employed and give your energy to the value of your knowledge and skill. You can also exchange money and get someone else's time and energy to help you. There is always a balance and a movement within the triangle.

BALANCE AT DIFFERENT STAGES

The employee stage

The trouble with a career, job or self-employment status is that it can feel like life is in balance, but the fun is missing. This is because the time triangle is so big that energy, money and you

DIAGRAM: THE TRIANGLE OF VALUE

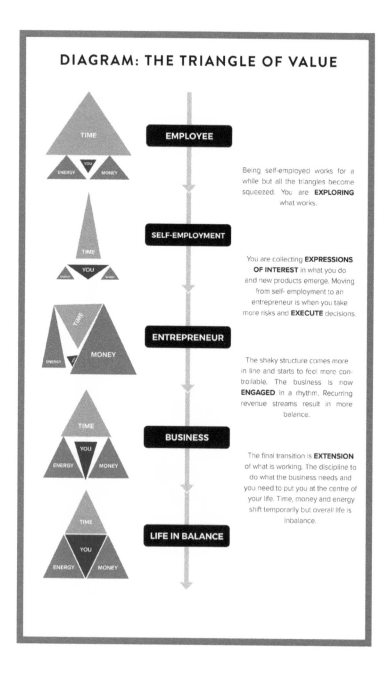

EMPLOYEE

Being self-employed works for a while but all the triangles become squeezed. You are **EXPLORING** what works.

SELF-EMPLOYMENT

You are collecting **EXPRESSIONS OF INTEREST** in what you do and new products emerge. Moving from self-employment to an entrepreneur is when you take more risks and **EXECUTE** decisions.

ENTREPRENEUR

The shaky structure comes more in line and starts to feel more controllable. The business is now **ENGAGED** in a rhythm. Recurring revenue streams result in more balance.

BUSINESS

The final transition is **EXTENSION** of what is working. The discipline to do what the business needs and you need to put you at the centre of your life. Time, money and energy shift temporarily but overall life is inbalance.

LIFE IN BALANCE

are all out of relative proportional balance. Eventually, this catches up with you and you lose your spark.

The self-employed stage

Self-employment is a move away from the selling-your-time-for-money scenario, but at the heart of self-employment is a time-based outcome for clients. Everything in the triangle becomes a bit smaller to begin with, and you initially get some time back or at least the control and priority setting of your own time. Being self-employed is a lot more about you. What can you do for the world? What value can you provide? Your energy shrinks a little when you are starting out because you are trying to get something going and your confidence is affected, which zaps your energy. Income is slow to start with, there is always something you can invest in, and if the business is growing it needs capital. There is always less cash than ideal.

The entrepreneur stage

This is messy, so much is going on it's difficult to keep things on an equilibrium and all together. Something slips as one triangle gets too heavy and squeezes other areas of your life. It's all about work and making money but it's not fun. You are not getting the personal satisfaction you need. Your mindset is that you need to consistently be pushing the business forward because you are thinking: *what if it all falls over tomorrow?* That's certainly how it felt to me. There was a hamster wheel that keeps on turning and you can't get off. Your time is all upside down, your energy is squeezed and you are in danger of burning out. You have some systems, but there is no flow or integration, it's all a bit ad-hoc. Some assets have been created, but the business isn't using them in a systematic way.

The business stage

Moving from an entrepreneur to a business requires rhythm. The business finds a level of sustainable performance, there is some cash to invest in systemisation and the business has a pulse to it; it operates without you in some areas. Assets are created that do some of the work, fully integrated systems bring leads in to the business and deliver consistency. Delivery and operations start to become smooth and flow.

The life in balance stage

Life is in balance when the business doesn't need you to do anything other than lead it. There are assets in the business fully integrated and performing at optimum levels. It's not just you, your time and your knowledge.

WANT TO LEAVE THE "TIME FOR MONEY" TRAP?

This book can help you avoid your time for money trap. This is something I help my clients do in a range of sectors. I have perfected the recurring income challenge. I don't want to ever retire. I don't fantasise about living in another country for months of the year because I love business, and I love my business. That only comes from a place of security and without struggle. I sleep and money comes into the bank account, literally, not six-figure sums but nice one, two and three thousand sums of money overnight. It is amazing. I can help my clients realise their brilliance too. I can help them plan for a time when they are not fighting for one-off clients. I know exactly what a customer is worth in our business. I know my customer's lifetime value to me.

WANT MORE FUN IN YOUR BUSINESS?

I am an accountant and I have seen first-hand businesses that I worked for lose money. I have run my own businesses that lost money. It's no fun working in a business that loses money. It's stressful, everyone is blaming everyone else. Profitable businesses get to invest in cool stuff that brings more business in. Staff have time and space, with more money there is more fun. The best business models I have seen use an asset or get a customer that gives a recurring revenue stream with a high profit margin.

Let me give you some personal examples:

Not fun – I ran a chain of five pubs that had small individual sales at a high cost without any predictability.

Not fun – I worked in a food manufacturer that had small high volume sales at a low margin.

"

You can't be everywhere and do everything; there comes a point when you run out of energy. You can become burnt out very quickly.

"

A little fun – I did retainer-based client work based on results, not time-based value.

Fun – A quarry business that used the asset of the stone to keep a steady stream of high value income coming in by using that core ingredient and packaged additional things the customer wanted, to make washed stone, concrete, mortar, bitumen to make tarmac and labour to deliver a full contracted solution.

Fun – I own a property business that has rental payments coming in every month.

Fun – I own an online training course that has membership fees coming in every month.

Many business owners and career professionals reach out to me for my help to escape their job, business and the clients they don't like. They want to sack their job and fire their clients. Ultimately, they want to make more money with less hassle and have more fun. They want to be recognised for value.

If you are a small business owner there is a limit to how many clients you can service without putting yourself under strain.

You can't be everywhere and do everything; there comes a point when you run out of energy. You can become burnt out very quickly.

You don't want to refuse any work as you have had to work so hard to get it in the first place. You don't know when the next lot of work will land on your desk, you may become quieter soon, so you need to accept everything that comes into the business.

A lot of start-up entrepreneurs start with a service-led business, which is a "time for money" danger zone! They sell their time doing things for other people, or, as one of my friends would call it, "doing mates favours for money". Once your initial network is used up it becomes far more challenging to keep selling services. If you have a high demand service like cleaning or gardening, then eventually you run out of hours and need to take on another person. To scale, you need to take on even more people and you need to sell even more hours. The larger you get, the more staff problems you have, the more people go off sick and you amplify your own problems by having 30 other people's problems. You need a product that doesn't need your time and earns money without you.

Instead, you need a product that delivers value to your customers and is unique to you. Why does someone pay you for your time? Because they want you to achieve something for them. They want your experience, advice and knowledge.

Nothing is more fulfilling than to help others achieve the things you know. We are in an age of community and sharing and the more you share the more people will gravitate towards you as someone who can help them.

MY BACKGROUND

I used to work as an accountant in business, exchanging my time for money. I was miserable. I found work-life balance and managing a career was stressful and demotivating. It got so bad that after two decades, and on the verge of a breakdown, I left my corporate role for good.

Before taking the leap, I had held various accountancy roles and I specialised in industry and management accounting, helping businesses understand their figures and how to make more profit and why certain products and services were unprofitable, and why they weren't making more money. I am not the type of accountant that puts together your annual accounts. I spent 20 years of my life making sure I was available on the 1st-7th of any given month to analyse why the business wasn't making the money that the shareholders thought it should.

I didn't just fall into accountancy. I worked hard to make my accountancy career happen. I completed my final accountancy exams in six months whilst running a pub and restaurant, holding down a full-time job and organising a wedding. I get stuff done and I make it happen.

I have completed around 240 month-end reviews for businesses. I have calculated businesses' products, services costs and prices. I have analysed profitability across customers, products, channels and services. I have worked on added value product businesses, where one core product has different services and value added to it to serve different customer needs. I have reviewed millions of pounds' worth of business capital investment projects to determine the additional profit and if the business should invest their capital. I have seen high volume, low margin and one-off product businesses suffer. A business needs good, highly profitable products to survive. Having high profit margins means you can afford to win a client. A lot of this knowledge has informed my philosophy and models of generating recurring income streams.

READY TO BREAK FREE?

Your knowledge is worth an absolute fortune to you but it's unlikely you've ever realised this. Why? Because you think you've been selling your time, but the truth is you've actually been selling an outcome of what you can deliver all along. Your know-how, your experience, upbringing and qualifications have made your knowledge unique, and this makes it irreplaceable.

The advantage of putting your knowledge online is you are using your time to generate benefit and value for more than one customer at a time.

Something special happens when you can leverage your time and help others:

▶ You become energised

▶ You can reach more people and customers

▶ You have more fun

▶ Your profit margins increase

▶ You have more money

Ultimately, this means you can help more people. If you are leveraged and can help many people by giving them just a small amount of your time, then you will have more energy for all parts of your business and life. In serving more than one person at a time, your energy and value is magnified, it organically grows.

Small business owners suffer from:

▶ Burnout (always at a client's beck and call)

▶ Only taking holidays every couple of years. Even then, they end up paying twice for their holidays as they are not earning whilst they are away.

▶ No cash to grow the business

▶ No cash to hire help

▶ No cash to bring consistent leads in

▶ Cash flow ups and downs

▶ Clients who don't pay on time, or the full amount

▶ The repetition of the daily grind

If any of this feels a little like your business, then you are missing recurring income streams from productising your knowledge.

ANYONE CAN DO IT

I had to change the way I worked to escape the time for money trap, which I will go into more in the next chapter. The focus of this book is how you can avoid the time for money trap to productise and sell your knowledge as an online course to create recurring revenues. The course assets in my business earn high five figures per month; regardless of what I do the money comes in whilst I sleep.

CHAPTER 3

ARE YOU CONSTANTLY AT YOUR CLIENTS' BECK AND CALL?

"Yes! Sorted, you're in business. Oh no!
You still have a job!"

ANON

HAVE YOU WORKED YOURSELF INTO AN UNEMPLOYABLE CORNER?

If you are self-employed or run your own business, you have a lot of responsibilities, perhaps children and a family to support and you feel pretty unemployable right now, but some days you joke about getting a job again. That little voice in your head howls with laughter. You have a self-employed job (which really stands for J.O.B. just over broke) and you just work for clients now instead. Why would anyone re-employ you? But you need money to pay the bills.

You may have already taken the huge step of becoming self-employed. It's official, you are employed by a mad person (you!) who can at times be a bit irrational, potentially stubborn, sometimes a genius and most of the time a headless chicken. The other bad news is you are probably unemployable now. Lacking the skills to sit at a desk and be sent to meetings all day long, you would probably explode at your boss and tell them where to stick their job. The good news is it's all about you, you are in charge.

The number of times I've heard entrepreneurs and self-employed people discuss being unemployable now they have their own business and that they work harder for less money. They are still employed by their clients and not much has changed except they get less sleep and more to worry about. I have made the mistake of selling my time to clients and thinking that because I didn't bill or charge for my hours on the invoice that I wasn't selling my time. In reality, I had just put a fixed fee on the invoice instead and taken all the risk of overrunning. The outcome I was selling still needed my time. I burnt out really quickly. My business flew for a few years and then I crashed and burned.

ONE PRODUCT, ONE CUSTOMER

I see small businesses making mistakes when they do all the delivery in their business to keep costs low. Entrepreneurs make the mistake of not applying any systemisation. They have a client and they sell them a consultation or project outcome and then they deliver that. This means that they have lots of one-to-one clients and they do all the heavy lifting of delivering in their business.

There is an expression commonly used of "working in the business not on the business". This basically means that business owners get so busy delivering that they don't look up and realise how inefficient they are. They've been so busy delivering, now the sales funnel is empty and they have to go out and

"

Being an entrepreneur can be financially tough too. As an entrepreneur, you need to cover all your overheads and tax bills, then you get paid or maybe even spend that money to bring in new clients.

"

sell. Not only does this result in burn out of the entrepreneur, but then the business starts to contract and shrink. Customers experience a reduction in the service level because the owner is doing everything themselves, which results in the opposite of what was intended.

If you are doing all the repetitive boring stuff yourself, it is quite common for entrepreneurs and experts to lose their passion. The repetition, the energy drain and the fatigue of doing the same thing over and over eventually pulls on energy sources and it's not much fun. Perhaps you could use a combination of online resources and systemisation. Can your clients do more for themselves?

HAVE YOU RUN OUT OF TIME TO SELL TO YOUR CLIENTS?

The challenge with a service business is that the only way to grow turnover is typically to increase the size of the team to deliver the service. The larger you grow, the more staff you have and the more overheads and structure you need. You need managers to manage the people delivering the service. Then you have overheads to cover so you need to sell more and then you need more cash to bring in and acquire customers, you need a sales team. It's a vicious circle.

Team and staff come with their personal issues – you need more HR, you inherit the team's problems, you need more structure, larger offices and more management. If a member of your team needs to take a day off to care for their family, you know that their priority is their family and they will take the day off regardless of your business priorities. That's the way things work. But particularly if you are a small employer it is really tough.

Being an entrepreneur can be financially tough too. As an entrepreneur, you need to cover all your overheads and tax bills, then you get paid or maybe even spend that money to bring in new clients.

Bringing in new sales and worrying if the big client will pay their invoice on time can all affect how much money you make. It's not much fun waiting for cheques to arrive to find that your VAT bill is more than you had thought. I sympathise with the worry about finances, it's particularly difficult if you don't have a cash buffer. Sleepless nights worrying about paying the bills and where the next sale is going to come from becomes a thing of the past once you have enough regular income to cover the basics.

HAVE YOU MIS-SOLD YOUR TIME TO YOUR CLIENTS?

Correctly pricing your services is a challenge, particularly at the start of a new business when you want to get going and make some money from new clients, but at this stage you are unlikely to know your true costs. However, I see service-based businesses wrestle with the challenge of how to switch to value-based pricing. For example, I worked with an architect who charged based on a percentage of the building value he was designing. This system ensures he is accurately pricing his services, but not all industries can define their value so succinctly.

On the other hand, I know a nutritionist who charges £150 for an hour consultation which takes 6 hours – 1 hour for the meeting, 1 hour post-meeting follow-up and 4 hours' research and report writing. That works out at just £25 per hour. She has spent years and years crafting a career which she is passionate about, and then getting experience to really help her patients. Yet it is difficult to value the outcome of having a healthier lifestyle financially. Say her patient earns £50/hr, if she saves them 20 sick days a year, it could have a value of £8,000. Yet they still only pay £150 for the consultation. There is a huge gap between the value and price.

Having an online course allows you to disrupt the time for money trap.

Productising your services with some online methodology and perhaps some one-to-one time allows you to package your services into a product for a set fee. Selling more of your time is exhausting. You promise yourself you won't take any more clients on until you've cleared the backlog, and then one more pops up and asks you nicely. Worrying that potentially there will be a quiet period around the corner, you take the client and become stressed, overwhelmed and worn out.

ARE YOU OUT OF THE HONEYMOON PHASE?

Normally, once you have started your business. While working for yourself was fun for a while – you probably got some clients and then got paid, proving your concept and your ability to deliver for clients. You are still impressed by your ability to keep your head above water and you are making ends meet. Some months it's fantastic and then you have a VAT quarter and you realise it's not so great anymore. Where's all the cash gone? Are you realising your dream? I don't believe anyone goes into business to earn less than six figures, but in reality, they do. Are you making as much money as you set out to? Are you feeling pretty ordinary about things?

ARE YOU AT THE MERCY OF DEMANDING CLIENTS?

Perhaps you have clients that you hate working for, but you need another income source to be able to fire them. Some clients you just know you should never take. It often comes with the culture of the organisation. I worked for one client who had a funeral industry-based business. A lot of their customers were very upset. They had become accustomed to the *shout at the supplier* relationship if anything went wrong, since, if they made a mistake, this is what their emotional and upset clients would do to them. The client dealt with all of their supplier relationships in exactly the same way; they would shout and stamp their feet. The consequences were that all suppliers drove their prices up with the client because they were so difficult to deal with. In an ideal world I would have cancelled the client's contract with me, if I wasn't relying on the income from the business we were doing with them.

When you have a baseline income coming in, you can choose who to work with (you are free to say no to those clients you know will be a nightmare) and you can also push your prices a little higher. This often creates a sellers' market because customers sense you aren't so desperate and you will only work with them at a higher price. It creates such a powerful pull for new clients rather than having to push to get new clients. It's a massive win-win.

DO YOU HAVE TO TAKE ON HUNDREDS OF CLIENTS TO SURVIVE?

The more clients you need to make your business work, the more complex it becomes. Especially if you are providing a regular service and you need to communicate with your clients each year.

I remember when I was looking to leave corporate life, I was adamant that I didn't want to take on lots of 1-2-1 clients. The responsibility and reliance on me as a one-man band felt overwhelming. The obvious choice for me was to start an accountancy firm and take on lots of clients. I was not keen on managing 150-200 individual tax returns. That felt like hell because you are responsible for so many clients.

ARE YOU IN THE BURNOUT PHASE? (BE HONEST)

It's pretty normal to hit a burnout phase. Why? Normally because a number of things collide. You don't see it coming because they are all fairly small:

▶ Your marketing starts to work.

▶ You have taken on more work than you can handle.

▶ Your VAT returns, corporation tax bills and self-assessment tax bills are all starting to hit at the same time.

▶ You get big new customers.

▶ You haven't had a holiday for a while.

▶ You're just at the point where you could afford a holiday or a member of staff.

▶ You take on more complex cases or work.

▶ Your reason why has been forgotten.

▶ You work at the weekends, early in the morning and late at night.

▶ You get an unexpected bill.

▶ You get customers who don't pay you.

▶ You get a pain of a client that you knew you shouldn't take but you did anyway.

▶ Some element of your personal life has suffered since running a business.

▶ You missed a school play, you forgot a friend's birthday.

▶ You haven't done anything for yourself for ages, you've dropped hobbies.

▶ You've stopped exercising while you got the business off the ground.

▶ Your house and office are the same place.

Part of making a change is accepting you are where you are. It's not wrong or right, it just is. Recognise that it is important to forgive yourself for what has happened in the past. It's neither useful nor helpful to hold onto what has happened before. If any of these problems are happening in your life and business and perhaps resonate with you, then read on, I have some ideas that will help you.

PART TWO

RECURRING INCOME
(YOUR TICKET OUT OF THE
"TIME FOR MONEY" TRAP)

INTRODUCTION TO
PART TWO

Recurring income is the backbone of any business. In Part Two, I'm going to show you exactly how recurring income works and what it can do for your business.

In this section, you are going to understand the features of recurring income and why it has become more important that businesses have recurring revenues available to them. Really, as an accountant, I should have realised this earlier, but it has taken me years to appreciate the power of recurring income.

An asset, according to Google's dictionary, is "a useful or valuable thing or person" or "an item of property owned by a person or company, regarded as having value and available to meet debts, commitments, or legacies".

In accountancy there are lots of rules about when an asset is an asset. For our purposes, an asset is anything that can help us do the work of the business and generate money. It's like the elephant in the room for me. Having worked in many multi-million-pound businesses, it is only in hindsight that I recognise that those businesses had these assets: knowledge and physical and digital assets.

The best assets are unique and have a certain quality that is appealing or solves a problem in a particular way. For example, I worked in a quarry business whose stone had a unique quality of being very slip resistant, this made it excellent for motorway and race track construction. This made the asset more valuable and gave the income stream a unique channel.

Essentially, your knowledge is the same for you, it is unique; you will have experienced unique mistakes and successes. If you start to position that your knowledge is an asset, there is a change in your mindset. Instead of thinking about how you can use that knowledge to sell your services, now you think about the revenue stream off the back of it.

In my consultancy business, I was also trading assets, but their lifespan was short (approximately 1-2 years). I would calculate how to save a client money and then implement and deliver the savings. I would invoice a percentage of savings once they were delivered. The asset, in this case, was my valuable knowledge of how to save the clients' money over the next 1-2 years. The asset was mine and I carried out the work and implemented the savings at my risk and expense. At the time, I didn't realise what I was doing but it made my life more comfortable because I had a recurring income stream that was reliable for the next couple of years.

"

Like a hungry animal that constantly needs feeding, your business needs cash to exist. Your online course can help support you, it can give you some breathing space when times are tough.

"

I discovered recurring income when I realised the great cash flow you could get from property and renting out property. There was no need to go out each and every month and get new sales, the tenant takes a room and then you don't have to do too much each month except collect the rent. We don't have to start renting all the rooms out again each month, there is a recurring income for that asset. You just have to provide a good value service. If people get what they expected: a fresh, modern, clean, warm home with washing and cooking facilities, with repairs sorted quickly and promptly, then your customers are happy. Customer service is about providing what the customer wants. Property is not passive, but it is leveraged.

I don't believe anything is truly passive income. Passive income is normally the result of having earnt a sum of money and then getting a return on it by putting it into high interest accounts or shares. Even then, the original sum is the asset that earns, not the income from it.

Online courses can generate recurring income if you structure them correctly. The asset is your knowledge and, thanks to technology, we can put it online and make it available for your subscribers in a systemised and easy way.

An online course is a digital asset that can deliver over and over. Digital assets are great for being very scalable and, once created, can be sold over and over again. The growth is about customer acquisition. It becomes a predictable path.

Recurring income from your course will give you some cash flow security. It is very powerful. I am passionate about helping small entrepreneurial businesses develop revenues for their courses from their subscribers or clients. I know what it was like to need to earn £2k-£5k per month and have to work hard to find it.

Like a hungry animal that constantly needs feeding, your business needs cash to exist. Your online course can help support you, it can give you some breathing space when times are tough.

Leveraging assets to earn money is smart. It's like compound interest because over time the asset earns more than it costs and keeps growing and can be invested again and again. It's the recurring income that keeps coming off the assets that is liberating. It enables investment in the product and asset, but also gives freedom from the time and financial burden of instant and service-led income streams.

In this part, I'm going to show you the power and freedom that building a recurring income stream can give you.

CHAPTER 4

THE JOYS OF A RECURRING INCOME

"To obtain financial freedom, one must be either a business owner, an investor, or both, generating passive income, particularly on a monthly basis."

ROBERT T. KIYOSAKI

WHAT IS RECURRING INCOME?

My definition of recurring income in my business is: income from a customer who will buy a product or service from me for a period longer than one month, whereby the payment structure is automatically set up at the initial sale point.

The best type of recurring income is from asset-based products. An asset-based product is something that has been created or exists that can deliver value to a customer on its own merit. It may require repairs, maintenance or refreshing but it exists without you or your time. There will always be some effort and work required.

HOW LONG DOES THE INCOME RECUR FOR?

I don't ask customers to sign up to a product or service forever. The biggest commitment recurring income product we have is an online course that has lots of legislation changes and because this is updated regularly, some subscribers stay on the product indefinitely.

"

A business is a living thing, it is made of systems, processes, rules, manuals and leadership. There is no one business that can operate without human interaction.

"

WHAT IS PASSIVE INCOME?

The Wikipedia definition of passive income is: "Income result-ing from cash flow received on a regular basis, requiring minimal to no effort by the recipient to maintain it."

Passive income is different as it infers a financially rewarding forever relationship without any work. I struggle to define any-thing as passive income based on no effort because there is either work up front or work during the process of pretty much anything. A lot of people falsely expect they can do absolutely nothing to gain a passive income. That's why I quite like the Wikipedia definition, as it at least mentions minimal effort.

I much prefer the idea of leveraged income to passive. Lever-aged implies there is heavy lifting to be done at the start and although it doesn't have to be all your effort, there is income at the back end of the initial effort. That effort upfront levers the income at the back end. Passive income to me implies there is no value being transferred.

The job of a business is to create meaningful value that people want to buy.

A business is a living thing, it is made of systems, processes, rules, manuals and leadership. There is no one business that can operate without human interaction.

There is no such thing as a passive income business. Passive income does not exist, even when creating an online course there is work to be done. Businesses are about creating value that a customer is willing to pay you for. If you are just looking for passive income and don't want to do anything to achieve it then I don't believe the market will pay you.

However, building a recurring income takes the pressure off each month. Most businesses start each month trying to sell their products again from scratch, which can be exhausting and energy draining.

If you have a lot of one-off project sales in your business that take effort to land and deliver, having your income secured with small sales can mean the bigger stuff is more fun because the pressure is off. One of the challenges with having a model where the sales are one-offs, is there is no recurring income which means that your cost of delivery and cost of acquisition of sales is very high.

Businesses without a recurring income base often start the month from zero. They may have tied up lots of marketing spend and have built their reputation over many years, yet they are still not able to get their customer to buy more than once from them. Think of how many times you are going to make big purchases from a car dealership or an architect. There are many business that rely on one-off large sales. Once they have finished the month, they have to find the next month's customers.

Whereas in a recurring income model, you would need to lose every customer or subscriber to start the month from zero. This is an important point. You will still need to sell each month, but you have a baseline, a start, the hungry cash monster of your business is not starving because there is some cash coming from existing subscribers. If you do a couple of things each month to sell your products, then it is unlikely you will lose all your income in one go. If your members are receiving value each month plus you are adding new people all the time and your churn is low, then your number of members should steadily grow. This provides security and stability.

WHAT ARE THE BENEFITS OF A RECURRING INCOME STREAM?

Benefit 1. Financial

Regular money

In a world where more and more of our costs and purchases are monthly, it makes sense to have regular monthly income to match regular monthly outgoings. People work for their salaries once a month and normally match their spending to their costs. Businesses are very similar; purchase invoices get settled once a month and then people pay their bills from their sales. Subscriptions and memberships have a rhythm about them that is great for businesses to rely on.

Good business valuations

If you are ever looking to exit a business, a recurring income stream gives you excellent cash flow and therefore your business valuation. Regular, provable, backed up, recurring income is a huge boost to business valuations.

Predictability in cash flow (my favourite)

A good recurring income model helps businesses build a predictable cash flow. It would be very unusual to lose all your members in one month. Therefore, it builds great cash flow that you can, over time, come to recognise as being £5k per month, £10k per month, etc.

Small sales values and likely future purchases

A subscription is a nice small sale (there is little resistance to people starting up on your subscription programme). You can have a low-level entry trial period that starts off at £9.99 or even free and then goes up to the full price after a month, perhaps to £99.

Rhythm of fun

No returning to zero each month. Perhaps the biggest underlying benefit that supports all of the other benefits, is your customer is expecting to hang out with you and your business for a while. Your sales will not return to zero every month.

There is something about having an income that has a similar pattern and rhythm to costs that makes business more fun. If you have all your overheads covered by your recurring income, then your other more sporadic or "lumpy" sales, as I call them, create great cash and capital opportunities.

Benefit 2. Sales

Good proof of concept product

A customer can get to understand your value really quickly with a small, bite-sized product. When they like what they see, they can buy more. This creates a buying culture, not selling. I once heard a friend talk about a supplier who he thought really got what he wanted and understood where they were going. Instead of offering them a small sale of a strategy day, the supplier put in a six-figure fee proposal. This immediately turned off my friend and he never ever did any business with that company. Not least perhaps because the trust they needed to spend £100k is different to spending £100.

Creating a small, affordable sale that gives good value is often a good strategy to upsell to big ticket items later.

Builds trust

Customers need a small product to trust you first. Trust is built upon time and an understanding of values. If you share with your subscriber how they can do something ethically then you will demonstrate the value of good ethics. If a customer understands your values and trusts you after spending a small amount of time with you and your business, they can feel comfortable they can refer you to anyone else. Trust enhances customer relationships. Trust can be worth a lot of referrals and future sales.

Upsell pipeline

When a customer has consumed all of your content, they now want more. People want to buy stuff off you. Yes, it's true. Often when a customer really gets into a subject or expert and is fascinated by their topic of knowledge, they will want to gorge on your products, content and services. This shouldn't be a massive surprise to you, I hope. If you were at all like me, you'll have gone through several phases of pop star idolising as a teenager, buying every book, record and magazine and pasting every newspaper clipping of favourite popstars to the bedroom wall. Your customers want to follow and model your success.

Once you have a raving fan in your product chain, then we can move them into bigger and side purchases.

Avoids sales demotivation

If you are constantly looking to cover your overheads and costs by generating one-off sales, you and your team are likely to reach a point of sales demotivation. A business needs to generate lots of leads and interest to fulfil its sales process. Good marketing should deliver leads into a business. If the majority of your sales are one-offs, then it becomes exhausting to keep delivering new customers into the business.

Marketing Return On Investment (ROI)

If you have a good recurring income, then you can afford to acquire a customer at a higher cost and avoid spending out on leads that will only buy from you once.

"

Once you have a raving fan in your product chain, then we can move them into bigger and side purchases.

"

There is always a cost of acquiring a new customer and profit is eaten up by the huge marketing machine needed to generate lots of sales.

Benefit 3. Customers

Affordable

Recurring income products can be priced quite competitively because of the recurring nature of the product; the customer can spread their affordability over many months. Therefore, monthly charges can be lower than perhaps a full project cost or a one-to-one coaching program.

Addresses the gap between high motivation and low budget

Some customers are so highly motivated for your solution but would not be able to afford your 1-2-1 time, so previously would not have spent any money at all with you. However, they can afford a cheaper product such as an online course. The reason you are able to sell at such an attractive price is because you leveraged your time, spending it to build the course initially, and after that, you have very limited further costs. The process of providing learning in this way is much more efficient and cheaper for you, so you can charge less. This then gives you the opportunity to address high motivation and low budget customers.

Benefit 4. Product

Clarified content/offering

To make a productised version of what you do with a customer 1-2-1 or in a project solution, you will have to break down what it is exactly that you do. Much like creating a set of instructions for clients to carry out their own work, you are creating the instructions and methodology in a way that has mass appeal. This creates intellectual property in the product that you develop. It forces you to recognise what outcomes you achieve and how.

Fine-tuned methodology

Your subscribers and customers will give you feedback. That feedback will be useful to identify successes and failures in method, understanding or execution. There is an opportunity to test and measure the results of clients and improve the methodology. You get more feedback and the product improves over time. The product is then more valuable to your customers because it becomes better.

Repurposed content

Some products can be used in multiple ways. Creating a recurring income product can help you identify others, or you can package your product into an one-time lifetime, access all areas sale. There are multiple opportunities to build out from your single course, e.g. you can create:

▶ Tester products

▶ Full access all areas products

▶ VIP products

▶ Digital plus 1-2-1 products

▶ Group many-to-1 products

▶ Blended online and live content

Benefit 5. Resulting Outcome and Freedom

Simply put, recurring income gives you more money and more fun. You also have more time and more choice, choices about whether to take on more clients or shut the office for a two week family holiday!

Security & freedom

Security and freedom are directly opposing words and don't show up very often together. It is this dichotomy that makes online courses and recurring revenue models so attractive because they deliver these not normally seen together qualities and give us this contrariness. The reason that secure freedom can exist is due to the existence of the asset and the leverage that it creates. I found freedom in my life from delivering recurring income streams from my businesses. Due to my personal circumstances, I needed my time to spend with my family, so our income had to come from a source that didn't require lots of my time. Life is so much more fun now; our main income sources are all from recurring revenue streams that don't require our time.

Time freedom

Recurring income to contribute towards or fulfil your expenses and overheads frees you to go and do things that you want to do with your time. If you spend your time making money, there is no leverage to increase your income to achieve time freedom. You work harder and harder and typically don't move forwards or spend more. At some future point you won't want to spend all your time earning money, you will want to be retiring, not feeding a cash-hungry monster.

Creative freedom

The security of a recurring income enables you to breathe and make more purpose-driven choices. No longer will you be sitting behind an income vehicle you don't want to drive. I hope you make enough money to have a positive impact in the world and make it a better place for everyone.

Fun

It provides more thinking time and gives you the freedom to consider options and what the business should strategise. Thinking time for the owner and business allows results to come in and for the business to develop and trial new products, experiment with a few new marketing ideas, etc. It allows the business owner time to create, rather than being stuck in the selling then delivering yo-yo. The business and the owner get their mojo back.

If you have left the salaried, paid by the hour job, you might recognise yourself as working for a lunatic (that's you) and you might even feel you have failed, and to top it all off you are probably earning less per hour than you were in your old job. You're broke and it's not much fun.

What would you really do, if you could? If I gave you the solution to earn more than enough money, how would you finish this phrase "so that I can..."? It's not about the money, it's about the freedom and time you can buy yourself.

CHAPTER 5

GENERATE RECURRING INCOME WITH AN ONLINE COURSE

"Don't let your learning lead to knowledge. Let your learning lead to action."

JIM ROHN

WHY PEOPLE LIKE LEARNING

There are many reasons why we all learn. Some people love it because it gives them more power and confidence to act. Some love to learn new things just because they love learning. They love absorbing new content from books. I love reading and the process of learning. I love business and the opportunities it creates, and I love to understand new and different things in my niche.

You see new opportunities when you've learnt something new. Learning creates a new perspective that can improve lives. Many enjoy learning and the challenge that learning creates. There are people who just love to learn because it means they can earn more income and increase their return on investment, and avoid making potentially expensive mistakes. You can learn quicker and earn more, faster, when you learn from others. I have been through a learning curve in our business and created online courses that generate high monthly cash flow. I've made mistakes and tested and measured many strategies.

Human nature draws us to partner with someone who has the knowledge and experience, so that our learning is quicker and costs less. Learning together is far more beneficial than working it out on our own. I am going to show you the way to create your online course, subscription and membership that will save you money but also get you earning money fast. My goal is to get you earning five-figure months from your digital assets and escape the time for money trap forever.

WHY ONLINE COURSES WORK BETTER THAN LIVE EVENTS

Better for the attendees

Online courses can have a deeper impact on people's lives than attending a one-day workshop, where a lot of the theory and the amount of content goes over people's heads. Most one-day courses are about 4-5 hours of content. People forget up to 90% of the content if it is not recalled more than once.

Most people leave the event or classroom and are immediately consumed with travelling plans and checking messages and emails and never get the course material or their notes out again. Therefore 70% forget the material within 24 hours and after one week it rises to 90%[1]. Most experts want to transform people's lives, they want their mentees to get results. Your online course can have a deeper impact than a 60-minute keynote speech. You can build in repetition in your course to help your students learn your content.

Many offline courses struggle to retain students through the course. The Research Institute of America found that this is not the case with E-Learning. Online courses have increased student retention rates from anything from 25% to 60%[2].

And added to that, IBM found that participants learn five times more material in online learning courses using multimedia content than in traditional face to face courses[3].

Better for you

I have run live events and I find that typically only 20% of the room buy any upsell or further programmes with us and so the customer lifetime value (LTV) is low. If we sell someone an online course, then these people have a much higher LTV. They naturally buy more from us because they have spent more meaningful time with us and there has been an impact (or at least some beneficial learning) in their lives from the information they have learnt.

If you are an expert, keynote speaker, consultant, influencer, thought leader or trainer you probably have to travel around the country to give your talks. This costs time and money. You have to fit in with other events and arrangements. Online courses have transformed my business and helped reach a huge geographical customer database and are more scalable in my business than anything else I can do.

As more and more former employees become freelancers and join the self-employment game, the more skills are required. There is now a new requirement of "lifelong learning". This skilling-up is crucial to evolving working environments. As the technology and tools we use every day get better, so do the skills that we need to use them.

Lifelong learning is now crucial to continued business success.

THE GROWTH
OF ONLINE LEARNING

- 50% of subject knowledge acquired during the first year of a four-year technical degree is outdated by the time students graduate, according to one popular estimate[4].

- More than 33%, or a third, of the desired core skill sets of most occupations will be comprised of skills that are not yet considered crucial to the job today[5].

- According to statistics from Coursera, online learners were at 10 million in 2014 and had trebled to 30 million in 2017.

- E-Learning is forecast to grow by over 20% annually. According to Forbes, the E-Learning market was $107 billion in 2015 and is expected to reach $325 billion by 2025[6]. The key factors that are favouring the market growth are: flexibility in learning, low cost, easy accessibility, increased effectiveness by animated learning.

- 300 hours of video are uploaded to YouTube every minute with users watching 5 billion hours of YouTube videos each day[7].

- Ted talks have over 13 million subscribers on YouTube at the time of writing this book, with very high growth rates.

- 70% of millennial YouTube users have watched a video to learn how to do something[8].

WHY A QUICK YOUTUBE VIDEO ISN'T ENOUGH

However, neither YouTube nor Ted talks have yet replaced schools, universities or colleges, despite the information being mainstream and free. We recognise that individuals need learning at their own pace and speed. The need is situational. Your knowledge and solutions cannot be taught in a 15-minute Ted talk. Ted talks are normally ideas, thought leadership or inspirational case studies. YouTube video is more entertainment based or practical, which button to click, etc. Learning requires repetition, further application and explanation of concepts and relevance to individuals.

WHY GOOGLE ISN'T THE ANSWER

Google anything and you will come up with a million differ-ent answers, and how can you tell they are right or wrong answers? You can't.

Objections to E-Learning are based on the fact that you can Google anything for free to find out what you want. However, despite the searches being micro-specific, with one question answered at a time, there is also the huge assumption that you have to know what the question you are asking for is first. If you don't know what you need to know, then how can you Google something you don't know? You also don't know the order of what to do next. Beyond a simple solution, Google is only useful to find key people or businesses that can solve your problem.

GOOGLE

- A lot of Google searches are thought to use algo-rithms that rank older web addresses and con-tent that has more engagements first. This means you are unlikely to pick up the latest thinking and trending ideas and will probably be shown some-thing old and possibly out of date first.

- A #1 position in Google's search results receives 18.2% of all click-through traffic. The second position receives 10.1%, the third 7.2%, the fourth 4.8%, and all others under 2%[9]. It's quite possible if you know what you are doing to optimise SEO for maximum click-throughs. This means information and knowledge shared is based on the commercial and marketing value of the data.

- 44 billion GB of data was created per day in 2016[10].

- 463 billion GB of data predicted in 2025 by IDC[11].

- 16-20% of queries that get asked every day have never been asked before[12].

- The amount of information is also so overwhelming it is difficult to find the specific answer you want.

- Data and information are created on the internet, social media and text messages.

- Devices are a huge source of the 2.5 quintillion bytes of data we create every day – the internet of things is producing an increasing amount of data[13].

- There were 3.9 billion internet users in 2018[14]. Up from 1.024 billion in 2005.

- Google has over 5.2 billion searches a day[15].

- If a particular piece of content has had histori-
  cally loads and loads of clicks, then that piece of
  content is going to race to the top of the Google
  platform. Google becomes a popularity contest,
  but what is popular is not necessarily what is best.

THE FUTURE OF LEARNING

E-Learning and community sharing has the potential to change
the world and help struggling families, men, women and children. What if we could teach the world about disease preven-
tion and treatment? What if we could share optimal farming
techniques to assist in food production? What if we could help
all those who experience trauma after a catastrophic environmental event (like an earthquake) to overcome the stress and
trauma? There are so many possibilities. E-Learning has so
many opportunities for good in the world.

In decades to come, learning will not be led by governments
but by communities who want to share their experiences and
successes.

Wage growth has stalled worldwide, and I believe this, combined with automation, is why businesses no longer value
modern education outputs.

Modern education is not cutting it because it lacks focus on
subjects that are relevant to business. The world is becoming
more and more entrepreneurial. More businesses are set up

every day than ever before. Businesses use a global work-force to deliver their services. Cheap and talented labour is now available in all businesses with outsourcing websites like Fiverr.com and Upwork.com.

Modern western education is expensive. Universities are charging thousands in fees to their students and the education system needs to change. Think how great it would be for our children to learn about financial models, legal structure, lead-ership, money management, methods of finance, investing and savings, the legal system and stocks and shares.

Business owners and entrepreneurs don't have the knowledge and skills they need to learn quickly and avoid the common pitfalls. They learn through trial and error. Mistakes cost money and slow down progress. If you have ever done anything well or successfully then you have the potential to write a course and product you can share.

The world is a lot smaller than it used to be; you now have a worldwide market in your smartphone. There is no need to work in the traditional way any longer. You don't need any specialist skills to access the technology. There are now ded-icated platforms that do the hard work for you. Share your insights and knowledge across a worldwide audience, this can all be done for next to nothing.

CHAPTER 6

NOW IS THE PERFECT TIME TO CREATE A DIGITAL ASSET

"The perfect time to start something never arrives START NOW!"

T. HARV EKER

WHY IS RIGHT NOW SUCH A GOOD TIME TO CREATE AN ONLINE COURSE?

There are many reasons why online courses were such a success in my business. I believe that now is the perfect time for you to write your product and maximise the returns from it. There is a little window of opportunity that I believe will be around for the next 5-10 years but not forever. I really believe that now is the best time because:

1. **We don't want to wait.**
   We are all more programmed than ever to receive instant gratification and information. Your customers are impatient; they want the information now. They want your content. Therefore, your customers do not want to wait six months for your availability, time and attention.

2. **We want to skill up and catch up.**
   Information about the world's most successful people and businesses is so much easier to find. This means we are so much more aware of our relative position, success or lack of knowledge. There is a tendency to feel knowledge poor. We can see that success can be achieved but not how.

3. **Technological advances.**
   It's now easier than ever to make a course, basically you could easily do it with a smartphone and an internet connection.

4. **Your customers are ready and waiting on social media.**

   Facebook was only created in 2004. Businesses have yet to take advantage of the true power of the size and scale of Facebook. There are over 3.2 billion users worldwide, including your next customers. Social media is able to target customers based on their interest and behaviour, this is powerful laser targeted marketing, making it easy for you to find and target people who are likely to be interested in your course.

5. **We are all subscribers.**

   We have all become much more engaged in the idea of renting services and products. Ownership comes with the challenge of upkeep, updates and maintenance. Renting gives us a much better way of controlling our costs. We are all able to pay as we go for a service and not be burdened with ownership costs. This has trained us all to pay monthly for something. This is a great reason to create an online course that has a membership structure and pay as you go features.

6. **Instant ROI.**

   You can create a digital asset that pays you back almost immediately and offers you a huge return on your investment. Therefore, I believe in the next 12 months it will not be difficult for you to earn a lot more money and have a lot more fun by creating digital assets. If you take the steps set out in this book, you can become one of the highest paid experts or creative leaders in your industry. Of course, you will need to invest time into the initial set up, you will need to overcome setbacks along the way and be prepared to amplify success when you see it.

OBSTACLES TO COURSE CREATION THAT JUST DON'T EXIST ANYMORE

I love business and I love learning. Setting up online courses, subscriptions and memberships was the obvious business for me, but I had to wait for the right timing.

The reasons why I had to wait were because of the lack of skills I had that technology has now replaced.

Old Problem	New Solution
I can't code membership or course websites.	Membership and online course websites now available on low monthly subscriptions.
I don't have a secure payment portal to collect subscription payments.	Payment sites like PayPal and Stripe are widely available and cheap.
I need specialist high tech equipment like 4k or HD cameras.	These are all now built into smartphones.
I can't use social media to raise awareness of me and my business.	Social media can now be used to promote your business for free to your network.

Old Problem	New Solution
I don't have technology to broadcast my message.	Webinar software, slide shares and live streaming allow you to present and pitch to your audience online across the world at low cost.
Beyond Friends Reunited, I don't have an effective way to connect to individuals on social media.	You can connect with as many friends as your profile will allow on social media. You can message each one individually.
There isn't a need for my knowledge.	Now we are all knowledge hungry. It's easier for us to compare ourselves with the successes of our friends on social media. We see others do things we want to do and achieve.

ARE YOU STUCK IN THE PAST?

In 1989, Tim Berners-Lee and his team invented the World Wide Web. In Feb 2004, Mark Zuckerberg released Facebook to the world and social media was born. Social media and the internet have created a world of potential. However, business typically takes a long time to take on board new technology. We are just seeing the business world embrace social media. Almost a third of businesses (31%) admit to being slow to adopt technological innovations, according to a study by TomTom Telematics. The findings have been compounded by the revelation that a third (32%) still use paper to store business-sensitive information, and that more than half (53%) use spreadsheets.

You must embrace the new technology because poor but well-educated countries are; you could find yourself surrounded by new international competitors. Countries like the Philippines, India and South Africa, who speak good English, are able to operate worldwide businesses. Building brand presence and awareness on social media is essential for a business to survive in the next 10 years.

ARE YOU MAKING THE MOST OF DIGITAL?

Given that we now have fantastic off-the-shelf software that we can purchase and smartphones that are as powerful as computers, there has never been a better time to adopt the power of social media, the internet and the sharing culture of the world we live in today. All of this smart technology has collided and enabled the small entrepreneur to set up, track, analyse, test and measure a successful business online. The digital entrepreneur can create their own digital assets and be anywhere in the world.

Digital has a fantastic way of revealing the return on investment of an activity. You can collect data at any point in the process. This has naturally led to the death of traditional marketing and sales methods. When you can choose to spray the market with generalised advertising, it can be difficult to track which section of the market reacted and even which advert

"

_Digital assets earn money whether you
are working in the business or not._

"

worked. We are now so much more aware of what it takes for a customer to make a purchase. We know our click-through rates. We know the awareness the customer needs of the brand and the product before purchase. We can also track which pages get the most views, which advert the customer clicked on which platform, it's all trackable and traceable.

THE JOYS OF DIGITAL ASSETS

To liberate your business from the reliance on yourself or people you need to create assets. Most people focus on selling more of their time. There is no scale in your time. Eventually you will run out of time or burn out.

Digital assets, however, such as online courses generate income and save costs. Assets have their own life; they are not dependent on you. An asset is something of value that can produce outputs that can be sold or deliver a service. An asset that is digital, such as a set of blogs, e-book, e-brochure, video, professional slide deck, can be leveraged digitally to work on your behalf. They are all like little salespeople running around on your behalf telling your customers how great your business is. If you have an asset that can deliver your training and advice directly to your customers, this will save you time. The work involved in creating an asset normally involves up front work or an exchange of value at the beginning to create the asset. The time it takes to create the asset and the work involved is relative to the return. They must be created and normally take longer to create in the beginning. The asset delivers value to you or your customers, that either saves you time or energy and saves you money or earns you money.

Digital assets earn money whether you are working in the business or not.

The market will pay you for the value you or your assets provide. The trick is to find a way of selling this that is commercially viable. Using an online course means that you deliver value in an effective and cheap way. However, there is still work to be done. If you are in the wrong market or industry and hate what you are doing, then creating an online course is not guaranteed to fix that. You could still be amplifying something you don't want to do.

Customers want to buy from you, and you will seldom give them enough opportunity to buy all they want and completely exhaust all of your value to them. If you can give customers a way of consuming your content and value in an online format, perhaps a course, membership or subscription, then you can build an asset of recurring income.

WHAT TYPE OF ASSET COULD YOU BUILD?

There are many types of digital asset you could build, and you will probably already have some of these or recognise them in the marketplace. Try and think creatively about how your knowledge and these types of asset could be combined.

To create an asset from your knowledge, skills and insights, you will need a product like an online course, membership or subscription. The list below outlines some of the most common products in this area:

1. **Memberships** – access to a group, place, equipment, community, content or documents that you can only access if you pay your membership.

2. **Priority clubs** – exclusive or early access to something. You provide people in these clubs with information or products that nobody else can get.

3. **Online courses** – learning either as a one-off or on a monthly recurring subscription.

4. **Community memberships** – content is shared, and projects are celebrated across the group.

5. **Pure time with mentor memberships** – whereby members get regular time with you.

6. **Product memberships** – regular distribution of a product for a monthly fee. The Gin Club is a good example of a product membership, each month a new variety is sent out to members, with a magazine and some content.

All of these digital and physical assets are subtypes of memberships. Memberships are all about following a cause. It's a relationship and a brand. With memberships, you impart your wisdom to your customers. It's all about your knowledge, and your understanding, and your learnings. With memberships, you want to give your customers a solution to their problems or a remedy to their pain.

Memberships need to have significant value to your customers. One of the problems with memberships is churn. Churn being where members might unsubscribe at a later stage because they're no longer using the product or getting value from it.

Good memberships get great engagement. Some of the ways you might increase engagement is by providing a regular platform of topical and relevant content to keep the customer up to date with new legislation, topical news, new scientific research, studies or learnings from your industry. Keeping your customers up to date with these kinds of things will ensure you have a highly engaged community, and people could potentially become customers in other parts of the business.

One of the benefits of a membership is you can actually provide a low-level product and cost per month but actually have the opportunity to upsell your customers onto additional products and other services, thus increasing the lifetime value of your client. Lifetime value is an important metric, it helps you understand how much money you can spend acquiring leads.

A membership online course has many win-wins for you and your business. Everything should improve.

CHAPTER 7

TIME TO PROFIT WITH ONLINE COURSES

"To copy others is necessary,

but to copy oneself is pathetic."

PABLO PICASSO

HOW MY EXPERIENCE LED ME TO AN ONLINE WORLD

It has taken many years of trial and error to get to where I am today, writing this book of learnings, mistakes, small wins and experience for you. I have books stacked up in my office, on my bedside table, on my kindle and on my phone. I have spent hundreds of thousands learning and then honing my learning. This includes money and time I've spent on educating myself with books, coaches, courses and mentors, the expensive mistakes I've made, the blind alleys I've gone down. I have developed and perfected my system over many years. I have created £400,000 of courses in my businesses, plus upsold to people who started out on my courses and helped a range of people in all sorts of business sectors to build recurring income streams through online courses.

There are other online course experts that have big launches and sell to big lists and make millions, but they are likely to have spent millions on marketing and affiliate commissions and may have spent years working up to that stage. I'm not here to tell you that you can be just like them overnight. My methodology is focused on creating transformational monthly recurring income from existing small lists and your current audience.

As mentioned, I started out in accountancy where I worked for clients in businesses that made everything from tarmac to chicken nuggets and cider. I have also worked for businesses that sold consultancy services in engineering and information in procurement.

Every business I have ever worked in did something very clever. They took some information and turned it into a product.

That information may well have been the right recipe for concrete that goes into a bridge or a lintel for a building. That information could have been how to manage a chicken nugget production line that produces a bag of 20 chicken nuggets every six seconds (literally as fast as you can count them dropping on to the production line).

I calculated profit and losses in many businesses, and the businesses that were the most profitable always had very high profit margins. These were typically on products that were unique to the business, products where there was some quality or feature that the customer valued and paid for. My take away from all that experience is that where you have unique experience and knowledge nobody else can compete with you. The profit margin in an online course is also high. These two factors are key to the success of an online course.

1. Information and knowledge that is unique to you.

2. Low cost of delivery and high margins mean it's easier to profit with a few subscribers.

As my knowledge and my husband's knowledge of property investing grew, we started to mentor people on how to achieve a good income from property. Having only just got our family time back after my husband left the police force, the last thing we wanted to do was to spend every weekend training new property investors.

I knew we had to put the content online. It was the only way we kept our time.

WHY THE SUBSCRIPTION MODEL WAS THE ONE FOR ME

At roughly the same time I read a book called *The Membership Economy* by Robbie Kellman Baxter which explained that "The smartest, most successful companies are using radically new membership models, subscription-based formats – and explode their market valuation – in the most disruptive shift in business since the Industrial Revolution."

As soon as I read the book, I knew that a subscription product was the answer and that if we didn't adopt that model, it would be extremely hard to sell one-off courses and programmes for flat fees. Not only that, we would be on a hamster wheel of sales. I'd seen it in so many of the businesses that I had worked with as an accountant. The course was designed

"

Once we knew we could replicate the success with other industries, it was then obvious that we had a winning formula.

"

to be over 12 months, so we decided to split the payments into monthly chunks.

PHASE 1 – OUR FIRST COURSE

Together, my husband and I wrote our first property course in late 2015. We created a webinar to get people interested and promoted it on social media. The first webinar only had 15 people. We made two sales from that first webinar. At this stage we didn't actually have the course recorded, we were just promising that the first month's content would be ready by the 1st of the next month. This gave us a month to deliver.

Over the following twelve months, we moved forwards, a few sales at a time, with more attendees on our webinar and smarter social media adverts. We were frantically recording content, selling it and keeping it all going.

Initially, it was confusing. Sometimes 40 people showed up on a webinar and then at other times only 20, with no apparent reason why. Slowly, I learnt to track webinar attendances and email conversions. I slowly added the building blocks of testing and measuring into the model.

After a while, it became clearer what the average sign up rates were, who came from where, and what money could be spent to drive people on to a webinar. It became a little widget machine, meaning so much in at the top meant so much out at the bottom.

The more we spent on advertising the course, the more people heard our story. Despite having almost zero profile in the industry to begin with, gradually, through the course creation process and marketing the products, the profile of our business grew. Our customers talked about their successes and how good the course was, and awareness organically started to grow. I carefully said "awareness" and not sales because I don't think there has ever been a single instance where someone has arrived at our website and just paid their money straight away. There is always a process where they get to know the product and decide whether it's right for them.

Within six months of launching the course, we were achieving sales/sign-up rates of 10 people each time we ran the pre-sentation webinar and hit 30 members really quickly. Then we fine-tuned our marketing and improved our product.

PHASE 2 – WORKING WITH OTHERS

We then had people approach us proposing joint ventures. Basically, we could sell our product to their customers, and they would make a commission on sales. This was not something we had originally thought of but was a real game-changer for income levels.

I then approached other industry experts with expertise to sell. They had their niche knowledge and we had the know-how of how to get the product structured and sold in the market place. It was a natural partnership. This was amazing; before the second expert's product was written we had 20 paying subscribers on the list. We quickly reached revenues of £3k per month with this product alone.

This grew organically, whenever I saw expertise and a mountain of value and knowledge, I then approached the person to joint venture with us and share their story.

Once we knew we could replicate the success with other industries, it was then obvious that we had a winning formula.

It took me months to work out what we did quite naturally and build a model and structure for others to understand and be able to apply in their businesses. Once I had explained and discussed this a few times everyone asked me about how to do it and they wanted to learn my methodology.

I haven't operated in every industry. I can't guarantee that your industry will be different. I don't know if there are similar products that would compete with yours. I do know that if you are prepared to be authentic, tell your story and share your insights, you have the best chance to find success.

WHAT AN ONLINE COURSE CAN HELP YOU ACHIEVE

I run a community group with other online course providers in the USA and Australia, and whilst I haven't been able to evidence with accounts, I understand from one online subscription course product provider, they are making sales of $80,000 a month. This isn't all profit, of course; they may well be spending $79,000 a month on Facebook ads. I do know that we have traded as high as £21,000 per month and we are not spending more than £750 per month in Facebook ads.

The top level of your income does depend on the knowledge you have and the market that you operate in. I never set out with the belief that running online courses would be such a great income, it was designed to be flexible and fit in with our already busy lives and our other business interests. I realised that I could scale the numbers online with small sales values.

THIS IS NOT AN EASY GET-RICH-QUICK SCHEME

This is not a get-rich-quick scheme. It is not passive. Close this book if you think you could teach a few bits and pieces of knowledge and earn millions. It takes time to reach this level. If you write a course and stick it online on your website and expect to sell millions, then it will fail. You have to know your stuff and your knowledge should lead others to make their lives better and more fulfilled. If you have a business and help others make money, then you have the chance to create an asset of huge value to your business and bring more fun into your life. Recurring revenues are the dream of every business because they allow the planning of income and the ability to reliably forecast revenues.

To achieve anything, effort is required. It is the fundamental law of achievement. Achievement is not passive. It is not gifted. It is not received. Achievement is earned.

"Success is never owned;

it is only rented – and the rent is due every day."

RORY VADEN

BEFORE WE GET STARTED

If you are about to embark on changing your life and business for the better, then there are a few things you need to do to make that happen. The good news is that I have changed my life through trial and error, and so I have taken the long route. I can give you the benefit of my experience and you will receive the rewards much quicker than I did. So here I'm giving you a great shortcut.

The main problem is when are you going to start working on your digital asset. You've got to make the decision and commit the time. I find lots of people are ready to do this, they've had enough sitting back watching others do it and realise, "Oh, I know what they know and someone else is making money off it" or "Someone is using similar IP and mine is better, and people are buying it. Why can't I? I want to do it. I'm ready to do it", yet finding the time to do anything about it is a major obstacle.

"An object at rest stays at rest and an object in motion stays in motion with the same speed and in the same direction unless acted upon by an unbalanced force."

NEWTON'S LAW OF MOTION

Starting

There is something quite powerful about starting well. The better you start the more powerful the momentum. The better you can start, the more successful you are likely to be. I have started projects and let them slip for a couple of weeks, and then another project or something else comes along that takes my attention. Start well, commit to it and keep the excitement and momentum up.

Time

Find enough time to plan properly before you start. Plan out as much as you can. Don't worry too much about having a huge detailed plan, but the more planning you can do, the clearer your thinking will be. The clearer your thinking, then the quicker you can get your course to market. The brain is great at juggling thoughts, it spins the thoughts around and around, keeping them all alive. The quicker you can dump them out of the brain and on to some paper the better. The planning process will save you a massive amount of time. Try to find a plan to succeed by regularly putting aside a time slot to do some of the work you need to do. Get up 20 minutes early each day. Do 20 minutes at lunchtime. Plan what you will achieve in those time slots. Book a couple of days off to start the project, and get some content written and then recorded.

"Every minute you spend in planning saves 10 minutes in execution; this gives you a 1,000% Return on Energy!"

BRIAN TRACY

Worth ethic

This process is for the savvy businessperson who expects there to be some hard work. There is some heavy lifting at the front to get results at the end. But I will teach you a way to do this without having to spend too much time on it before you have tested your market. I will also teach you a way that will drag you to complete your course without having to use lots of self-motivation and energy; we will use the motivation of the results of your courses to move you forwards. This is not a magic wand. This is a blueprint for business, written for businesspeople that understand they've got to work at it.

You will need to commit to the process as your customers will be waiting for your content. In essence, I have tried to design this programme to stop you procrastinating and replace the need for discipline with accountability.

Mindset

I only want you to do this if you understand this is not for everyone. You will need tenacity. You will need to be comfortable with setbacks and failures. With a test and measure mindset, you can create assets of huge value.

The brain will sabotage you unless you can show it how reliable this new income stream might be. Obviously, it will be a while before the income starts coming in. Expect to have fears, doubts and disbelief. Your brain will give you lots and lots of reasons why it won't work: you don't have enough IP, your ideas are rubbish, you can't do it, you are not clever enough to earn £10 per month never mind £10,000 per month.

If you notice these thoughts come into your brain – and this might seem completely weird and nuts, but in my experience it helps calm the niggling self-talk – stop! Say out loud or in your head, "Thank you for protecting me, but I got this".

It's not easy to change and your brain's job is to protect you. You have to trust that it will feel uncomfortable and different. Keep moving forwards.

Systems

Everything you are about to do is about providing value; it's about detail and it's about systems. If you have order in your thoughts and actions, then everything else is taken care of. The absence of order creates overwhelm. Overwhelm creates procrastination and then nothing happens.

Like a butterfly that starts as a caterpillar then turns into the pupae, there is always a bit of an ugly middle stage. Change can be the same. I advise you to think about the outcomes and take one step at a time.

If you look at the construction of houses, with foundations, bricks, lintels, windows, doors, staircases and a roof all making up a home, think of the order and systems you create in your life like the building blocks of your dreams. I fundamentally believe it's impossible to be successful and happy without having small systems and processes in place that support you. What can you systemise to give you some time back so you can create some content online? Can you find a cleaner? Someone to mow the lawns? Do you really need to paint the house right now? Can you find someone to help you with some of the clutter? Outsource things that need to be done but don't help you get your course written.

Embrace it

Realistically, you will never find a 3-week gap in your diary to sit down and plan the whole process. There will always be stuff going on. Embrace the hustle of 20 minutes here and there, and the fact that you are right up to your deadline, or two days over. Just get on with it. Enjoy the moments of pulling it all together and don't stress when it isn't perfect, just keep going. You will get there. Trust me.

PART THREE

THE 3 PILLARS

INTRODUCTION TO
PART THREE

"Any fool can know. The point is to understand."

ALBERT EINSTEIN

INTRODUCTION TO THE 3 PILLARS

In my experience, there are three things that need to happen in order for you to get your online course, subscription or membership to be successful. Nail these and everything else will fall into place. In Part Three I will be showing you exactly how you can get these three pillars right to set yourself up for success.

"

I love the way my model helps small
overwhelmed business experts address
all the weak points of their business
and their own self-doubt.

"

I've seen it over and over again, a really good expert puts their knowledge online and expect it to walk out the door and come back in with millions. It's the pipe dream to do a really big launch and to sell millions. It's like expecting to write a bestseller.

I've also noticed experts trying to create their course in one big chunk of effort and procrastinating to the point that they give up and have a half-written course or idea out there. My model addresses this by avoiding the big effort testing bit.

I love the way my model helps small overwhelmed business experts address all the weak points of their business and their own self-doubt.

Most people are looking for time and financial freedom, give them those things and they will find their purpose in life. The 3 pillars model is unique in aligning your know-how whilst providing significant secure freedom.

If you have these 3 pillars in place, your product will be super successful and easy to deliver, sell and grow. You can repeat the process over and over. Once you learn the 3 pillar system, then you can grow a business that can really scale. Our products have had exponential growth due to the compounding effect of the growth of customers. You can always put more rocket fuel in the spaceship if you want to, and that's the beauty of this process, you can decide if you are going up to 40,000 feet or trying to break free from the atmosphere.

My model and methodology work because they have core principles:

1. Delivering value – USP & IP

2. Taking small actionable steps for you and your customers – Format

3. Commercial viability – Sales

People that struggle to sell their digital products have missed one or more of the fundamental pillars. I've seen over and over again, failing course owners lash out at the market, defend and protect their brand and become super aggressive. The trouble is, if you have designed something wrong and it isn't working, then you end up wasting your time and energy about a subject you care deeply about. It is difficult to let go.

The success of a digital product is not in how many pay per click ads you can get to convert but in how the product can be invested in, how you can get your customers to be successful, how your IP is packaged and how you let the market know about your IP.

In this part I will be fully explaining the 3 pillars to you, to set you up for success.

I have repeated the success of the online course model with others and my own experience. I've realised there are many hundreds of ways you could be creating an online course but, in my experience, to do this successfully you need three things that *have to* happen in a particular order. I refer to these as the 3 pillars:

Pillar 1. USP & IP – You need to know what your USP / IP is and that it is worth something to someone else.

Pillar 2. Format – You've got to have your content formatted and structured really well to support the basis of a really good subscription product.

Pillar 3. Sales – You've got to sell it.

These are the pillars of making a success out of your knowledge and they will enable you to make more money and have more fun with less hassle.

PITFALLS

Each pillar is equally important, neglect one and you will have one of the following problems.

1. IP PILLAR IS MISSING
Wrong content, customers don't engage in a meaningful way

These people have the right format and they're trying to sell it, but they've got the wrong IP. It doesn't have any traction; it's got no legs, people aren't prepared to pay for that knowledge. The wrong IP or the IP positioned incorrectly won't sell long term. It becomes a game of buying customers. Your customer lifetime value is low because they don't stick around. And your conversions are generally low. Testing your IP in the market on a pre-sale will help you develop an understanding of the value you provide. If your feedback is negative at this stage, you need to develop a better product. This is not about finding the best hook but about delivering the best value to your customers.

2. FORMAT PILLAR IS MISSING
Wrong format, burn out

These course owners have their IP worked out, they know it's worth something to somebody and they're selling it, but it's not in a subscription format that's going to make them a lot of money. Instead, what I see is people who are doing one hit wonder type things, which creates lumpy cash flow and the single payment can put buyers off so they cannot make regular consistent income. When structure is missing, course owners end up spending a lot of money on pay per click ads, thinking it's just a case of getting enough people to convert on a big sale launch. Some course owners do make massive incomes off the back of a big one hit sale, they do big style launches. This can be great if you have a big following or audience. I see fewer people successful at it because it needs your product to be fully written and completed for sale, people tend to procrastinate and never get anything out there. A big sales launch doesn't maximise the lifetime value of customers. Your cost of customer acquisition becomes very high relative to your product sale.

3. SALES PILLAR IS MISSING
All the content, no sales

The course owners in this category have got plenty of content and IP. They know it, and they know it's worth something to somebody because they're already seeing competitors selling courses in their niche. They've got all the bases of a subscription model, but they have gotten into the market. It's a classic case of "it looks great on the website". You can't design something, record it and expect lots of people to drop by your website. You can even try to tell people, but unless you do a sales presentation and pitch your product with an offer then nobody will buy. You have to sell and not just tell.

CHAPTER 8

PILLAR 1 – USP & IP

"You don't have to be great to start,

but you have to start to be great."

ZIG ZIGLAR

DO YOU KNOW WHAT YOU HAVE TO SELL?

Unpacking your value can be the trickiest part. You must find a way to productise your knowledge and insights. If you can solve a problem for people or businesses, then you will have a product that can deliver meaningful impact in the world. It's about changing lives and solving problems.

Consumer-Led Knowledge (Business to Consumer B2C)

Your knowledge might be traditional and best suited to selling to consumers. For example, you may be able to teach people about arts and crafts, health and fitness, or music, all of which form an excellent basis for an online subscription product.

Business-Led Knowledge (Business to Business B2B)

You may have a business area of knowledge that companies or small businesses would find very useful. If you do something of value in business, then this could be a way of monetising your knowledge into a digital asset/online course. The knowledge would be used in a business environment. Your customer can earn more money from your knowledge which typically makes it very valuable.

SOME CLUES TO YOUR IP

An expert is generally somebody with extensive knowledge or an ability based on their research, their experience, their current job and their business.

The important thing to consider is this: how does what you know solve a problem that somebody else has?

You are most likely to take your knowledge for granted, so think about some of the situations where your knowledge turns up.

The following questions might prompt some ideas for you to explore.

1. What subject(s) do you love learning about? Is there a subject area that has become part of who you are? What could you talk about for hours? Is there a particular subject on which you have read every book published, followed other experts in the same field?

2. How do you help or mentor your customers and clients? You might consult with them and be an expert in helping your customers reach a certain outcome and solving their problems.

3. Who do you hang out with? You might be part of a group of colleagues or you might have some kind of network that actually delivers value and has expertise and shares common understandings of your industry. You might also be deeply involved in your industry. You might be a member of an organisation or association and you might volunteer or speak at groups or in business forums.

WHAT CATEGORY COULD YOUR COURSE BE IN?

There are eight categories that cover the majority of courses. This is not an exhaustive list but will just give you some ideas:

B2B

1. How to run a business like yours.

This area focuses on how to run a business in a niche. It includes teaching business skills, generating more money for the business owner or helping people start businesses, e.g. *"How to run a high performing coffee shop"* is knowledge not normally available to start-ups. There are very few organisations that tell you how to run a business well. There isn't a university lecturer in the world that can tell you how to run your business like a top performer, because they are teachers; they have theory, but they can't tell you how to market and run a business well. There is no "traditional" information that is going to tell you how to do this. How do you become the top performer in your industry? Unless you figured it out yourself through trial and error you might never get to the top. The "how to" is valuable knowledge. Those who can copy and learn from others, earn the most money, have the most bookings, are fighting off the people that don't have the capacity to cope with demand, so they can charge top prices. The fact that you run your business and have sustained some success in your industry could be all you need to deliver your course – to share that knowledge with other businesses in your industry.

If you do business well in your niche industry, you have lots of great skills. A lot of successful people market and attract their customers very well and don't think twice about this skill. If that's you, think about creating a course about how you can help other people in your niche and business do it well too.

2. Skills for business.

This is a huge topic and the skills taught could be useful across all industries. Although this can work for traditional business skills such as negotiating, there is a huge opportunity with tech business skills from how to run a Facebook ad, how to use social media to grow your customers, how to write a good landing page. You can combine these products into one course, e.g. Social Media for the Construction Industry.

You might also use a piece of software in a unique and unusual way that applies to your industries and be able to put together a useful course, e.g. Photoshop for Wedding Photographers.

"

The important thing to consider is this: how does what you know solve a problem that somebody else has?

"

3. Investment strategies.

These are primarily for individuals who want to make money, whether that's in stocks and shares, bitcoin, trading, property, etc. How to make money is one of the top performing topics on the internet. Lots of people want to make more money.

Investment courses need to provide lots of "how", by which I mean strategies to help subscribers avoid making investment mistakes, mitigate risks and think differently about investing and money.

These make excellent online courses because the subscriber will make financial gains *and* avoid making financial losses/ mistakes.

4. Academic.

These enable you to become accredited with a qualification. Qualifications through a home study package have been around for a long time. However, if you have accreditation and the skills to deliver this content you can compete with establishments and provide students with great alternatives. The corporate market is the biggest single market in E-Learning and with Learning Management Systems (LMS) you can track employee participation and roll out key courses your clients want their teams to participate in. There may also be a course you could provide to your client for their staff to use, e.g. *"Organisational values"* or *"Key leadership team deliverables"*. Blended learning works well with corporate clients, "blended" being a mixture of some live one-to-many class-room-based courses and some online content.

5. Vocational.

These teach you a particular trade or skill such as carpentry. There is often a pay-off in extra income too. You learn more skills to earn more money, but it is a skill in itself, not just how to be a carpenter but how to use your carpentry skills to build a loft conversion for your construction clients.

6. Professional.

Courses that are designed to give your customers a qualification such as first aid, health and safety, understanding of legislation, etc.

B2C

1. Diet and lifestyle.

There is a huge range in this category for people who want to lose weight, eat clean, look good, get fit, build muscle, etc. During the research for this book, I discovered that one of the top ten YouTube search questions was "How to lose belly fat quickly?" Weight loss, fitness, diet are very popular searches on the internet. There is so much information on the internet about these areas, so it's absolutely essential in this category to be super niche and, subsequently, clear to your subscribers on the potential value of your course.

2. Personal development.

This is another broad category containing major self-help topics from how to manage your time better to how to rid yourself of anxiety. People turn to the internet for lots of solutions to their personal challenges and problems. An online course is sometimes perfect for someone with personal problems or challenges to overcome because they don't want to share it with anyone, they can get the help needed with discretion.

3. Interests.

These focus on purely recreational hobbies which range from the more obvious like playing the guitar and training your dog to more niche subjects such as the history of churches or painting cows. I love this category. It has worldwide appeal. Everything from cooking to painting, even guitar lessons. I know a photography course that generates £80k per month for the course owner. Typically, because there is no return on investment (i.e. people don't make more money as a result of your course), the pricing of this course is lower, but the members are more loyal and come in volume. The course content can be infinite. New designs, new ideas and new recipes can be covered month after month, so customers often buy lots of products and have a high lifetime value.

There literally isn't anything stopping you from designing a course about the moon. You just have to work out if you can reach enough people to make it worth your while.

If you feel you can provide value to someone and teach them particular skills and provide information that they don't necessarily get from anywhere else, then you've probably found your course. Don't worry about the market, just focus on what you are good at. We will test the market later, before you do too much work.

KEY QUESTIONS TO DISCOVER YOUR USP & IP

- Have I got IP that's worth something to somebody?

- What underpins my thinking?

- What are my ideas?

- What other existing products, content or blogs are available?

- What have I got already? What can I repurpose?

- What do I find easy that others find hard?

OVERVIEW OF USP & IP

1. I know what my USP and IP is.

2. I know if my knowledge is consumer or business led.

3. I understand what type of course I will deliver.

4. I am left with a number of ideas.

5. I find my know-how is unique because...

You have to work out what your IP is, and you have to work out if people think it's worth paying for. In summary, have you got IP that can sell? There is only one way to find out...

CHAPTER 9

PILLAR 2 – STRUCTURE

"Design is a funny word. Some people think design means how it looks. But of course, if you dig deeper, it's really how it works."

STEVE JOBS

DO YOU KNOW HOW TO BREAK DOWN YOUR KNOWLEDGE?

When you're structuring your online course or subscription you need to think about breaking the information down into bite-size chunks across a timeline and how people will sit down and learn your information. It may need to be quite progressive, whereby skills build up one by one. There has to be an element of practice, and the student fixing some of the skills and knowledge into memory and into their behaviour.

If you have a very functional product that requires somebody to do X, Y and Z, and there's not much content or information to teach, then you need to think carefully about how you might structure this into an ongoing product (once the subscriber has done Z, what do they need you for?). The key attribute we are looking for in structure is a product where the content can be spread across a number of months to create a monthly subscription. You can align your content into months.

The second most important part of your course is the structure. Structure is how the course is designed and the payment plan is created alongside this. For example, you might have six modules and deliver one a month for a monthly subscription fee. There are two types: "infinite" (which can always be added to) or "fixed outcome" (more on these below). If you want recurring revenues, you need a structure that places the content over a timeline. However, you can't expect people to pay you for the next 10 years if you gave them all the content on day one.

Infinite

Infinite content can carry on forever – there is always something to be added. For example, you might teach in an ever-expanding area such as the latest social media marketing trends, in which case you will never lack new material to create add-on products.

Fixed outcome

If your product is likely to be an outcome for the student, i.e. you are promising to get them to a certain stage, *"Pass your guitar grade 5 exam"*, for instance, then ideally the timeline should be 12 months. Any longer and subscribers don't understand why it needs to be so long. Any shorter and you limit the tail end subscribers who stay on forever because they will ask you to cancel their membership once they are through the majority of the course.

Your exchange of valuable insights and your story may be supported by lots of inspirational case studies. You may be able to supplement your membership with group video calls to support those that may be stuck or need support. It does depend on your product.

CAN YOU PACKAGE YOUR KNOWLEDGE INTO A CLEAR METHODOLOGY?

We want to get really clear on the value that you add, your process and your model that delivers and spread it out as content to your subscribers. It would be great to provide your students with a clear methodology. Think back to what you have done in your experience and what you would do if you were starting from scratch again. Break the process and tasks into manageable steps or stages that can be taught in a linear step-by-step fashion. You have to provide a structure for people to learn. My 3 pillars methodology helps my readers understand the important components. You may have randomly worked it all out from experience, but your subscribers need an easy way to understand you. Therefore, you will have to create structure, even when there is none.

START WITH THE BASICS

At the beginning it is a good idea to give a foundation (stops confusion and overwhelm creeping in) or consider some quick wins you could share. Ideally, you want your content to be relevant and easy to understand. Subscribers often want quick results, so think about what you could deliver in the first few months that would get them some quick wins. This will also create high engagement because once your subscribers are off to a good start, then they are likely to stay as subscribers for longer; the churn (the rate at which people cancel) will be lower.

A good foundation course such as *"Home maintenance for first time buyers"* or fast track *"Buy a house in 2-3 months"* or *"Turn your coffee shop around in 10-12 weeks"*. It depends how you want to structure the learning. You can release the content weekly or monthly.

A very good software platform for E-Learning provider is Kajabi – you can choose to release content on a weekly basis or on a monthly basis. But if you release your content over 10 weeks, you automatically keep people on the programme for over two months, because 10 weeks is at least two monthly payments. Your content is released weekly but you can charge monthly. This way you can prevent too much churn early on. People typically want quick results.

One of the first things I'll be getting you to do is write an outline of your product. But you really need to sit down and think about where the learning is for your key customer, who your target market is, and where your customer's problems show up. What we want to do is to get to your true value proposition.

KEY QUESTIONS
TO BUILD YOUR STRUCTURE

- What is your outcome? What are you promising to deliver?

- When somebody does your course, what are you looking for them to say they have achieved?

- What results do you get for people in your current business?

- Write down what exactly "it" is people get as a result of consuming months of your course.

- Have conversations with potential customers who will give you honest feedback.

You might need to reposition your ideas and spell out the outcome for your customers. Your course may have a fixed number of months or it might be an on-going structure with new updated content released each month.

Overview of the structure

1. Know your subject area well enough to understand the building blocks of the know-how you will teach in your online course.

2. Develop a strong offering that can be built upon.

3. Have good strong basics to start with.

4. Consider if your content is infinite or outcome driven.

5. Build a methodology alongside your content.

6. What problems are you addressing? How does your structure help your target customer learn?

CHAPTER 10

PILLAR 3 – SALES

"Approach each customer with the idea of helping him or her to solve a problem or achieve a goal, not of selling a product or service."

BRIAN TRACY

CAN YOU SELL YOUR KNOWLEDGE?

Selling is the oldest skill in the world, and everyone is selling all the time. We are all selling ourselves to our family, friends, colleagues and clients all of the time. Having a strong product and value proposition does not remove the need to sell, it just means you have a better chance of selling your product. Every business needs sales. You will never get away from the need to sell what your solution is to the world.

A lot of course owners fall into the trap of thinking they just have to put their best IP into a product and then they can sell it. If you think you are going to stick your course on a website and then it will just magically sell, you are mistaken. Your course is a digital asset, and you will need to explain the value of your products to your customers. Huge corporates with big branded and well-known products have sales teams; the job of their sales team is to sell their products. Brands like Rolex and Apple have salespeople that are trained in how to sell their products. Although their products are excellent, the products alone are not going to sell themselves.

Don't think you can just sit back and watch your sales roll in, the big companies don't.

Let me be clear, the financial freedom of a recurring income product comes from the fact that you don't have to sell everything every day. You don't start from scratch each morning as you have a recurring income stream where subscribers pay you every month. Our online course is deliberately built on a monthly subscription because this is how businesses and people manage their cash flow; they earn money each month and they have bills to pay each month. I could teach you to make a lot of money in a one-off hit, but this wouldn't be life changing, the recurring income that supports your lifestyle day in day out is transformational, whereas a lump of cash will be here today and gone tomorrow.

OVERVIEW OF THE SALES PILLAR PROCESS

The sales pillar process is as follows:

1. Find your audience, build trust, convert your audience into prospects.

2. Present your solution.

3. Address the problems.

4. Make the sale and take payment.

5. Test and measure the process.

1 – FIND YOUR AUDIENCE, BUILD TRUST, CONVERT YOUR AUDIENCE INTO PROSPECTS

You need to attract in leads and then you need to communicate with them to sell your products. You will need to find a way to reach your target audience, generate leads and create opportunities.

The psychology of human beings is such that we would much prefer to have security than to gamble on uncertainty. Your customers, who have only just come across you, will be reluctant to spend large amounts of money without being able to develop deeper trust and experience with you.

Whether you start from an email list, a live event, a webinar, a speech or a podcast you have to get out there and develop your sales funnel. The more you attract customers and subscribers to your business and feed it with good leads, the more will come out of the process and you will have made more sales.

2 – PRESENT YOUR SOLUTION

Once you have got in front of your audience, you need to explain why your product solves their problem so well. Selling your courses, memberships and subscriptions is about learning where your conversions are, where your audience hang out and then communicating your message and solutions with them effectively. Part of your marketing plan should be to deliver content and value to your customers, through under-standing their problems and helping solve them. By deliver-ing value and content you will get attention on you and your product.

To get the attention you require, you might use one of the following:

▶ Landing page

▶ Collect emails and send an email marketing campaign

▶ Webinar

▶ Live event

▶ 1-2-1 meeting

▶ Speaking events

▶ Published works upsell

In every example you might give something of value to your prospects for free, this could be a simple video or introductory module that you have or conceptual idea. You give enough information that enables the listener or reader to learn and take something of value from you. This builds trust and then you will have someone who is interested in your product.

3 – ADDRESS THE PROBLEMS

There are a number of ways your customers' problems are showing up in their world. You need to get a degree in your

"

As course providers, we need testimonial,

diagrams, stories and pictures to help

people visualise the solution

and the problems they can address

with your course.

"

customers' problems to help them. You must show them your solutions. If you are going to present your solutions, then you need to be addressing the problems that your customers need solving.

We all pay attention to different sets of problems. We all have common triggers that cause us to address our individual problems and look for solutions. When we are selling, we can use this understanding to help address the problems our customers are addressing.

Problems that your customers want to buy a solution to have the following attributes:

3.1 – Visibility

If your customers can easily see the problem and understand a solution will help, they will be much more likely to buy. The problem isn't small, it's obvious and not hidden. The same with the solution, if they are at all unable to see how the solution can help them, they will not buy. The clarity of the problem and the solution means your customer finds it easy to buy from you. If at any point the solution is not clear or the customer doesn't understand it, they are likely to abandon buying.

Complexity confuses the brain when it comes to buying. If the problem is complex, with inconsistent symptoms and signs, then customers are unlikely to look for any solutions and may not even consider they might need more than one solution.

If we don't own the problem, we don't see it as being in our control, and we will block it out and ignore it. When the problem or solution is not visible to us because a feeling of helplessness is something we all try to avoid, we place it out of mind. The more certain the potential solution, the more they can see and visualise the outcome, the more likely it is people will buy to solve their problem.

As course providers, we need testimonial, diagrams, stories and pictures to help people visualise the solution and the problems they can address with your course.

3.2 – Time-pressure

a. Short Term – Getting Worse Quickly

When the problem is getting worse quickly, the impact of the problem grows, the pain, the expense and the embarrassment all grow the longer the problem is left, so the customer is highly motivated to get it solved now. This is why, once you have presented your solution to someone, you should give them the opportunity to buy as soon as they are ready. Time kills sales because this group of problems is getting worse and a solution is needed quickly. If you don't provide this solution quickly, your prospect will go off and buy the next best thing.

Have you ever had toothache and you need to see a dentist but they are closed over the weekend, but the pain is so intense that you buy any remedies that say they will help numb the pain, like gel, liquids, sprays, etc? You buy them all until you can get to the dentist on Monday morning. If the pain becomes so intense you look for out of town alternative dentists or private dentists and will pay whatever you need to. If you have a solution that has a short-term impact, then make sure you help your customer and explain the solutions, and how your course can help them quickly and how you can address the long-term underlying causes so the situation is prevented in the future, so it's not just a temporary quick fix.

b. Long Term – Getting Worse Over Time

These gradual problems grow more significant over time and can be exacerbated by other factors. If the problem has signs that it is becoming more painful and getting worse, as a seller it's useful to point out what the signs are, so those in the early stages can take action quicker. Where a problem is stable or improving, the customer is less likely to buy as the problem is less urgent. It is like overeating – slowly but surely the weight creeps up and then the person becomes obese.

c. Ongoing Problems – It Can Never Be Fixed

What if something is so broken you will never have enough time to fix it, is it unfixable? This is where, as humans, we tend to give up; we cut out our problems and give up on them so that we don't go mad thinking and worrying about them. If something is a long-term, persistent issue we are more likely to put up with the problem and leave it. An example could be a political or environmental factor outside of your control. Or perhaps the loss of a loved one or child, how to cope with the trauma and the aftermath of this unfixable situation. Often the problem is so unfixable people don't look for solutions because they don't believe they exist. It is the pivot and the different perspective you can offer to solve the problem that is often the non-solution, solution.

Tell stories about how bad something has got to address the inertia and status quo that some of your clients might be in. Encourage those that have given up on a broken problem that there are alternatives, and the underlying causes or scenarios can be addressed with your solution. Your online course could address finding finance to get cash flow going, invest in some key sales deliverables and assets to generate future revenues.

3.3 – Status

Our ancestors have been around for millions of years and we have been around for about 200,000 years. Yet we still have the primal instinct of survival that means status is a sign of survival and continued chance of surviving. Status is anything that can keep us looking good to our friends, enemies, competitors, employees, family and loved ones.

Status is a sign of your significance or the value that you provide to the community you are in. Those that have value and are trusted advisers are guarded and protected by their community. Therefore, we all try and achieve significance and a level of understanding of subjects and knowledge. Nobody wants to look or feel stupid. Recognition is often a way of achieving status.

Your target customers might not know how to manage money, or have no idea how to have positive conversations or control their emotions. It depends how much they feel the problem is overwhelming them and the scale that they are having to face their problem. Some examples might be *"How to meet influential people online"*, *"How to win awards for your business"* or *"How to negotiate to win the deals you want"*.

4 – MAKE THE SALE AND TAKE PAYMENT

You must ask for the sale. Most people hate this bit. Asking for money for your knowledge may seem strange initially but this is crucial. If you are going to have any chance of helping any people in the world, then you have to allow them the opportunity to buy from you. Some people want to buy from you. I find it very frustrating when I want to buy something and there is a salesperson busy trying to tell me why I need their product, and I want to buy it, but they are not letting me in to buy.

You need a way of taking money in exchange for entering your course platform. Once you have some sales you can start investing in what works. You will start analysing things like the lifetime value of your customers to understand if your programme is actually growing. You can make some money, invest in marketing spend to acquire customers (Facebook ads, networking, Google ads) and time producing your product. Instead of going to zero every month. Then you can try and work out what is working in the customer acquisition process – how can you scale?

5 – TEST AND MEASURE THE PROCESS

To perfect the conversions in your sales process, you will need to do some trial and error testing (referred to as A/B split testing). This is where you have two versions of something, and you test the original A (could be anything to help a sale, e.g. a landing page, an advert, a commercial, etc.) against the alternative B, changing one variable at a time. Then you monitor the best results and keep the winner and stop the loser. The idea is to learn from what doesn't work. So don't give up because your first page doesn't work.

After, you start analysing things like the lifetime value of your customers to understand if your membership is actually growing. Growing could mean that customers stay on your course for a longer length of time or you are getting better at adding more people each month. You can then develop a process to make some money, invest in marketing to acquire new customers (Facebook ads, networking, Google ads) and focus on producing your product. You are building your recurring income and each month you should see better and better income coming through, certainly whilst you are acquiring your subscribers.

It's like a little miracle because really it is like compound interest, every customer you put on to your programme as a subscriber builds your income for the next few months.

If you know you are not a natural salesperson what can you do to improve?

The only thing you can do to improve is test and measure. Test and measure automatically requires you to be playing the game over and over until you know what works. In any football cup challenge or World Cup playoffs, teams are allocated into groups. The teams play against other teams in their group and then they play the winners from another group of teams, the overall winner is the team that has played out in every stage and group and reached the top.

To follow this analogy, you play with one set of conditions in each group, you pick a winner, then you take that element, technique or strategy and move forwards again.

PART FOUR

THE 5 Es

PART FOUR

n Part Four, I'm going to share with you my tried and tested 5 Es Methodology. Using this you will achieve online success with recurring income products. The objective of this methodology is to build up to five-figure income months. Each step has been carefully created to:

▶ Build a product that the market will love.

▶ Beat your own procrastination.

▶ Get your product created in super-fast time.

THE 5 Es EXPLAINED

The order that you do the 5 Es; you must work your way through the process in a clear, methodical way.

1. Explore

In this stage, you Explore your intellectual property, knowledge, skills, hobbies and look at your successes that could contribute to a solution to a customer's problem. You may have a passion or interest in a hobby that could form a really good online course subscription or membership site, or it may be more related to your career.

The other part of the Explore process is to recognise the assets and content that already exist, which could assist your product.

If you skip this stage, you might not have the confidence that this is the right IP (from all that you have) to take to market. Having confidence in your product and online course will massively improve your chances of succeeding. You won't be absolutely certain that you have found the right thing, you just might end up discovering your best ideas and opportunities too late.

The internet is full of information. Your customers want *your* experiences, know-how, learnings, wisdom, knowledge and successes.

The outcome of Explore is that you will have a level of confidence that you have an idea of what your course will be about to test in the market.

2. Expressions of Interest

In this stage, you establish whether there is a market for your product. Once a course subject is decided, most people go off and write the next 20+ modules and don't do anything else for the next few months. They shut themselves away and work for hours and hours on something that may have no traction in the marketplace. I also find that a product isn't really alive until someone is prepared to pay money for it: you might love your idea, but the market might not, you might be wasting your time. The 5 Es process is outcome driven so we look for customers to express their interest in your product by pre-launching the content and asking for early deposits. This generally means that the product gets launched quicker. You get to test your product in the market.

If you skip this stage you could spend a year working on an untested project without earning a penny, meanwhile, some-one else could come into the market and earn before you.

The outcome of Expressions of Interest is to have some early adopters subscribed, earning you £500 – £2k per month.

3. Execute

In this stage, you will write, design, record and produce your product. Executing and having customers on your product whilst you produce it gets you revenue from day one. Your product will change, and you can test and measure your sales pitch and process whilst delivering the content. If you have followed the previous step properly, this should be a heads-down process of delivering your content to your audience. You will also need to keep selling your product whilst recording the content.

If you skip this process you will end up running out of content and your sales will die. People have already paid a deposit and are expecting you to deliver in the timeline promised. You want to keep the deposits.

The outcome of Execute is to have your first module live and delivered to your early adopters.

4. Engage

In this stage, you Engage your customer, because getting them to stay on your course (and keep paying their subscription) will require your customer to get value from you. There are many ways to keep engagement high. It's about making the course better, tweaking content and perfecting the offering.

If you skip this stage, you will get a high dropout rate and you will need to find new customers frequently. It becomes a lot harder.

The outcome of Engage is to achieve an income of £2k – £5k per month.

5. Extend

In this stage, you Extend your product's reach and get it in front of as many people as possible. Hitting high monthly revenue targets is about getting your marketing working and building your profile. For example, you could significantly increase your results by working with an affiliate introducer, a JV partner, other industry suppliers and increasing pay for click and ad spends.

If you skip this step, you won't get the high-performance results that your product deserves.

The outcome of Extend is to achieve £10k per month.

CHAPTER 11

EXPLORE

"If you can just help enough others get what they want in life, you will have everything you want in your life."

ZIG ZIGLAR

WHAT IS EXPLORE?

The first step in our methodology is Explore. The reason why we Explore is because we want to find out what knowledge, experience, success or passions you have that could make a great product and help other people. Explore makes sure that you don't overlook or miss your most valuable Intellectual Property (IP) and Unique Selling Point (USP). Most people say, "Tell me what to do?", but before you jump in you need to Explore what it is you can do first. What do you have to offer? You might already have some clues about what your IP is, and we're going to be discovering them in more detail and testing it all out.

Nothing ever worth doing is easy. Creating products and assets will give you a fantastic return on your time and money. In the first few months of my first product, the business was taking £500 per month with a small list and a small profile on social media. After about three months it was earning £1000 per month and had 30 subscribers, which, by the way, totally blew my mind.

You're already doing something; you're already delivering value. You've got an established business or career, but your knowledge is not making you enough money. There might be a different angle on your knowledge than you were expecting, so please dig deep and write down anything that comes into your head. Let's get creative.

Most of us already have all the expertise and learning. We all take for granted what we know and have learnt. I know that you have learnt a lot of strategies along the way. You have a great deal of experience and great case studies.

WHY IS EXPLORE IMPORTANT AND WHAT HAPPENS IF YOU DON'T DO IT?

What can go wrong if you don't do the Explore step?

▶ **There is a weak hook for your product.** Basically, this means the need for your product is not strong enough or, put another way, your customers are happy to put up with their problem rather than pay you for the solution. If your product addresses something that your subscriber feels comfortable living with and can continue to live with then the pain point may not be uncomfortable enough for them to subscribe. For example, a course on photography to take better photos on your phone. Who is this for? Young people who use social media a lot. The problem? You tell them they need to stop using their phone and buy a fancy SLR camera. You've not solved their problem.

► **You have no Ideal Customer Avatar (ICA).** An avatar represents your ideal customer. You need to know them inside out. If you don't know your customer, then your marketing cannot target them and you won't be able to have a successful marketing strategy no matter how much you spend. With the hook, you know what problem you solve, now you need to work out who has that problem badly enough to pay you to solve it, e.g. you help retired people to make quick and easy family meals. The problem – retirees have lots of time. The solution – is counter-intuitive, retired people want to put a lot of time and effort into making family meals.

► **You don't solve customers' problems.** Worse, you don't solve any problems. You create a beautiful chocolate teapot. I identify the problem of my target market, I identify who they might be, but then I write a product that tells them why it's a good idea, I show them examples of a good product and I even point out the characteristics needed for success, but I don't tell them how. Perhaps retired people do want to cook meals that appeal to the wide age range of a family and they need inspiration, but you have solved a different problem and are helping them with quick and easy meals, which isn't their problem.

The Explore stage can take time and money to perfect, but time spent exploring your offer will save you hours in course creation and marketing. The problem I often see is that people don't explore their own personal knowledge and value properly. They don't do the work, but quickly decide to do something popular they've seen work elsewhere. Your USP has to come from you and help your audience. I've seen mentees write out their knowledge in a big subject list that fails to address their membership's needs.

CASE STUDY 1
Don't Compare

I asked someone I knew to become an expert in our business. I wanted to work with him to build a course. This man was somebody who I felt had a lot of knowledge, but he just didn't know what he knew. He had no concept of the value of his information to others. He wasn't really sure of how to monetise his IP. He had come to realise that he had a lot of knowledge, and that other higher profile industry experts were relying on his skills and knowledge. He was comparing himself to these experts and getting frustrated that he was being overlooked as a person of knowledge and influence. But he was sitting in the background just contemplating his value, waiting for someone to recognise his status and not doing anything about it, feeling powerless and undervalued.

A WORD OF WARNING: SHINY PENNIES

Some entrepreneurs have shiny penny syndrome, typically when their sales are challenged. A lot of new opportunities come along each and every day and it's a challenge to stay on track and focus on the current sales opportunities and work. It sometimes seems easier to sell new things. Shiny penny syndrome comes up when perhaps your motivation is low or you're feeling unsure about your market. Don't start this project just to have another unfinished project; having half-finished things is energy draining. Set the intention to do it and finish it.

Don't make the mistake of going off topic and don't go into new industries because you think they are the next best things. Be the best at what you can do. One of the common mistakes people make when they're struggling and looking for additional income is to change industry and to change their expertise. Understanding the language of your industry is paramount to you being able to sell your product. You are preprogramed with your industry's terminology and stories. It all helps you sell your products.

One of the things that Steve Jobs did when he came back to Apple was reduce the number of products that Apple sold. He reviewed his ecosystem of products and sales so that they focused on doing less things well, rather than lots of things badly.

All of these little things will really impact how you can sell your product and get traction with your online course. Your niche is where your sweet spot is. It's where you show up and it's why people will come to you for that expertise.

THE 6 STEPS OF EXPLORE

Step 1. Explore what you could teach someone

It's a good question. Everyone has valuable knowledge and wisdom gained over years of experience. We are all just a different mixture of experiences. There really isn't any area of knowledge that doesn't transfer to a course. To test my theory, I challenged myself to write a list of things that I thought *couldn't* work as a course. And the first thing I thought of was algebra. I mean, who wants to study that online? But then I thought of a course that could be sold to parents, *"Learn more about algebra than your kids, so they can ace their homework"*.

Nothing should limit your thoughts or creativity, find an angle to sell your knowledge in a unique way. You need to drag the ideas out of your brain.

Questions to help you Explore what you could teach

▶ Who struggles to understand what you know?

▶ Who could transform their business/lives and make more money with what you know?

▶ What have you learnt over the years and systematised into a routine?

▶ What are you comfortable doing?

▶ What are you here to do or achieve?

▶ How can you help others and improve their lives?

▶ How do you know that your knowledge isn't of value?

▶ What is your purpose in life?

▶ What feels easy to you that others overlook or find difficult?

▶ If you have more than 10 years of experience in an industry, there is something that is just second nature to you – what is it?

▶ What do people ask you to help with?

▶ What overwhelms others that you see as easy?

Some of you will know straight away what it is you want to teach others and be speeding off to other sections in this book to get some detail about how to do it. But slow down, this next section might make you hundreds of thousands of pounds' worth of difference.

Others might doubt their knowledge is of value, but what if you could inspire a generation to find their quiet moments in sewing a cross stitch, knowing it helps them to relax or find quiet time? What if you could show someone how to paint animals? The paint strokes, the lines, the shape, the beauty of the animals, the colours and the accomplishment of hanging your own artwork on your wall. Imagine how those students feel when they have done that? Given that this is a more recreational course, I think it's worth reflecting on what problems, hooks and solutions are involved here. An online course doesn't just have to be about creating wealth for others.

Your target customers have a problem that they want to enjoy a hobby but fear they lack some of the skills. They particularly love animals.

Problem: The customer is looking for an activity to enjoy and spend time doing. They are currently bored and lacking purpose, a little sad and lonely in their own time with nothing to do. They want to overcome lack of direction but find it painful to paint on their own. They feel that if it goes wrong the whole thing is a waste of time. They have no way of achieving a satisfactory outcome.

Hook: How to paint animals with a few hours practise each month and achieve results that you are proud enough to put up in your home, and your friends and family will admire.

Step 2. Explore your value

It is worth just thinking through your life, experience and story. What do you do that brings value to others? You will take this for granted. Your value is in the things that you do well. What is second nature to you? Chances are you've been doing things that just come naturally to you for life. You have interests and spend time reading, researching and networking with people in this area. You can spend hours doing something and time slips away.

Do you do things so well that others want to pay you for it? Some people will say things to you like "please do this for me? You're much better at it than me". You may need to think about this as so much of it is second nature to you, you won't realise how good you are at something. What comes so easy you don't even have to think about it. Accept your talents and that you are particularly good at something.

What have you done that you think most other people have never done? I ran and owned five pubs once and I think I could safely say that most people have never done that. Have you had challenges that most people would never have had? Have you had a challenge and made a success of your life?

Why do you do the job you do? At the beginning of a career, we all have dreams and aspirations of what a difference we might make. Where can you tune into this? I am passionate about helping other people change their lives and get more enjoyment out of their fraction of time on this planet. I only look to help businesses that have a positive impact on the world because I am passionate about people exchanging their time for money and giving you their only finite resource in the pursuit of money.

Questions to help you Explore your value

▶ Do you know you are competent at something?

▶ What results do you easily get for yourself or others?

▶ How do others refer to you? There might be some clues in the way people approach you or what they ask you to do for them.

▶ Are your customers getting a lot of return on their investment? If their return is high, then you can push your prices forward, put some of the repetitive stuff online and put your information online.

▶ Are you considered an expert in your industry?

▶ How are you a subject matter expert?

▶ Are you somebody who loves what you do?

▶ Have you made a success of a particular vertical in business?

Step 3. Explore your authentic self

I don't want you to go and research a subject to teach online, your value should come from your heart, it should be authentic. If you aren't sure what I mean, then I've got some pointers for you below.

Questions to help you Explore your authentic self

▶ What about yourself do you like most?

▶ What about yourself do you like and appreciate the most?

▶ What aspects of your life do you wish to see a change in?

▶ What are your fears?

▶ What are you grateful for?

▶ Are you happy doing what you are currently doing?

▶ What are you interested in but haven't tried?

▶ What are the most important things you've learned in life?

▶ Who inspires you the most and what is it that inspires you about them?

▶ How important is money to you?

▶ Where do you see yourself in 5, 10 and 20 years?

▶ What do you believe in?

▶ What are your values?

▶ What does your inner voice tell you to be true?

What common themes keep coming up in your life?

I keep looking at how different areas of my life have a common agenda or a common underlying cause. I left my corporate job to look for growth and control of my results. I felt I'd hit a glass ceiling and what I wanted to achieve could no longer be achieved in that corporate environment. I wanted growth of my salary, I wanted growth of my learning and understanding, I wanted to achieve new things, I wanted to learn new areas of the business, and none of that was available in my role.

One of the other things I enjoyed outside of work was gardening, growing from seeds. I love seeing seedlings develop and grow into beautiful plants. Once I noticed that, I realised I enjoyed the learning and growth of things in the world. One of the most important things I want to achieve in business is to keep growing. I track my net worth each month to make sure that number grows. I track the number of email addresses on our list. I track the growth in turnover of our businesses.

What are your personal values and beliefs?

Think about what is important to you. What do you believe is important to success and relevant to your industry? One of the great things is to find the crossover with a couple of values and look at how you can combine those two values into what you do; this helps you become super aligned with who you are. For me, I love learning and personal growth, so this goes hand in hand with selling courses and helping other people.

"

Lack of belief in yourself and your product is a weakness in any business model.

"

It's about changing other people's lives and helping them achieve their personal growth and their business growth.

Sometimes when you notice things that keep repeating, you might find an underlying pattern. Review how you might capitalise on these ideas in your business. Combining these two things is not just about making money for you, it's about intrinsically linking your business with your passions and your values. If you combine your business and values, you will create an ethical and strong business that has a compelling story.

Lack of belief in yourself and your product is a weakness in any business model.

Step 4. Explore how you can help people

What are your customers/subscribers trying to get done in the world? Everyone is busy and we all have different things we like to do with our time. Most people would like to spend their time doing the things they want to. Some are trying to fulfil their purpose in life and the more time they have to do the stuff that achieves this, the bigger impact they can have.

For example, the motivations of people taking their knowledge online could be:

1. **To make more money with less hassle.** No major clients or boss to be answerable to.

2. **To spend more time with their partner, children or grandchildren.** They will have leveraged their time through an online course to deliver the content without them.

3. **To overcome boredom.** Addresses their problem of repeating over and over their training, content and knowledge so they aren't repeating themselves.

4. **To add value to their industry.** Their course gives a professional methodology and approach to their subject.

5. **To develop themselves and invest in their knowledge.** Builds credibility and the designing of a methodology and models.

What is your customer trying to do in the world? For instance, when you buy a drill, are you buying the drill or the hole that the drill makes or even the emotion of the happy memories of all the photo frames that are hung on the screws in the holes that the drill made?

Questions to help you Explore how you can help people

▶ What are the most important reasons that people have for buying your product?

▶ What problems or needs motivate their decision to buy from you?

▶ What kinds of people are likely to have big enough problems to buy your product?

▶ What is the upside if the problem is fixed and solved by your product?

▶ What are the specific outcomes that these people seek?

▶ What features of your solution produce the desired outcomes of your target customers?

▶ What will the benefits be to these people if the desired outcomes are achieved?

Can you boost their income?

If you can solve a problem and help people earn more money from your course, your product immediately has a Return On Investment (ROI) for your subscribers, e.g. *"Boost your website conversions course"*, then you can charge more for your product as the outcome you promise can significantly improve the life/earning power of the participant. You're also likely to get more participants. For example, if the customer worked in a certain field, such as photography, help them earn more money by specialising, e.g. in wedding photography, pet portraiture, streetscapes, landscapes, etc.

However, the ability to earn more money isn't ultimately what people will buy; the purchase is always emotional, e.g. the extra things they can do with their family or travel plans they can make, the time they buy back or less stress earning that money. Think beyond the money.

Not everyone does everything for money. Be careful to look for the reasons for your subscribers to do something. Is it the enjoyment of a hobby or craft? Is it to develop a personal interest?

Can you buy them more time?

If you have knowledge that brings time efficiency or is a quicker way to do something, then this is of value.

Time freedom is likely to mean more to some subscribers than what they can buy with the money. It is the ability to choose what they want to do that can be a huge motivational force for them to engage in your product. The time your customers might be able to spend with their children or grandchildren – that can make a huge difference in their lives.

Can you help them add value to their business or career?

Adding value can increase your product's price in a big way. For example, offering an additional module to new leaders such as *"How to get started in a new promotion role in the next 90 days"* is a value-added feature to a course that is based on leadership.

Businesses and individuals are struggling to find a competitive advantage where skills can be recruited overnight and a task for a job can be completed and in your inbox before the next day's work has even started. Businesses are constantly searching to find a method of adding value to justify the pricing to a more globally connected customer.

People are looking to get an outcome when they work with you, they don't really care about the product.

Value is the difference between the price of someone's product and the cost of producing it. It's what the market tolerates as profit because there is an exchange of value. If you can help people find value in their own jobs or businesses through the information, inspirations, knowledge and experience you give them, they will automatically pay you, and keep paying you.

Can you help them develop themselves and invest in their knowledge?

Don't worry if what you're offering isn't going to result in more cash in the bank for your subscriber, there are lots of motivations for undertaking a course, e.g. imagine I was thinking of quitting my job in catering to start an online course on making your own wine. It's unlikely people will make money from the wine-making skills I give them, but they will enjoy it. You might bring a world of understanding to your subscribers.

Subscribers will pay you to be part of a community and belong to your membership. In this case, they may want to be part of your winemakers and wine appreciators club. We are all unique, but sometimes it can feel a little lonely if we can't share our passions and interests with others. Our partners and family might not get our interests and you can help someone feel like they belong in a small way to this world through your online course and subscription community. All winemakers together.

Step 5. Explore your niche

Remember, there is so much expertise in the world that you really need to niche to stand out. It's important to niche so that you can attract a market. But without your niche, it can look like you're an expert of all industries. The trust level goes down when you show up as lots of different things with lots of different expertise; you dilute your credibility. Smart people know you can't be a multi-subject expert. Work on a niche, it gives you a better marketing message and helps you attract more customers. For example, would you sign up to a course on cookery that was from an expert in public speaking or an expert in cookery?

Identifying a niche helps you successfully talk in your customer's language. A niche is something that specifically identifies somebody and identifies their problem. A niche will help you identify your target, but it won't limit your market. It does take a little faith. You will automatically feel like you are losing sales because you are niching but actually you are just clarifying your offering.

An HR expert approached me about their leadership training. We discussed whether or not that would be transferable online. We then realised they had particular expertise in helping people break through glass ceilings and overcoming their obstacles in the workplace.

Now, that is a much more powerful course than one that generically covers leadership skills. It's much clearer for the customer to understand if they can associate with that problem, and by doing that course they're going to get to the other side of their problem. Obviously, if you've got examples and case studies that support your success, then your overall proposition becomes more powerful too.

A course on gluten-free recipes for cake lovers is more niche than just general gluten-free recipes. A course on learning to code for the over 50s is more niche than a general coding course. The target is very niche, but it makes it so much easier for customers to identify that your product is perfect for them, and that makes them buy more. We want your ideal customer to identify with your product.

Remember: your customers are trying to learn something. They're either trying to perfect a skill, move forward on a problem they have or overcome their challenges.

Questions to help you Explore your niche

► What industry do you work in?

► What customer base do you serve?

► What is unique about your customers, products or industry?

► What are the barriers to entry for a new company or new expert?

► Who does your product benefit most?

► What sector is growing at the moment?

► What trends are developing in your industry?

▶ What has technology done for your industry?

▶ What information has changed the way your industry works?

Step 6. Explore who your customers are

You might have heard the phrase, "If you throw enough mud at the wall, some of it will stick". This is the idea that random selling will result in something sticking. Throwing as much money as you can at a problem and hoping that will solve it is crazy.

There is little point in throwing mud at the whole of the world, as everyone will see that no one is buying. Potentially, the fact that no one is buying will put people off buying your product. The whole world is not interested in what you have to offer, only your niche is.

If you have any idea of what your customer looks like, what books they read, you can create a customer avatar. Having an avatar will help you sell to your targets in a structured manner; because of their interests and their problems, your solution becomes immediately relevant to them.

You know your customer challenges and issues. There's so much noise in the world and it's becoming harder and harder to earn the trust of your customer, so think about what you are trying to achieve. If your target believes you can help with their problems and challenges, they will listen.

Questions to help you Explore who your customers are

▶ What does your customer want to do in the world?

▶ What are their values?

▶ For whom does your solution work best?

▶ Who needs your solution the most?

▶ Who would want to pay for your solution?

▶ Who would be able to afford to implement all that you are asking them to do?

▶ Which demographics have you seen take massive action?

▶ What were the common traits of customers who have had success in the past?

▶ What barriers do your customers have to overcome?

▶ Why can't they get help online?

▶ What piece of the puzzle is missing for your ideal subscriber?

▶ What books do they read?

O,

CASE STUDY 2
Don't Rush In!

I recently spoke to an experienced expert about putting the content together for an online course. We discussed their value helping big companies get their HR in order to manage out the people who were no longer suited to their roles, in the nicest way possible, so that they actually thanked them. Immediately, the first thought was to go and write this course: *"How to get rid of the bad apples in your business and have them thank you on the way out"*. It's powerful, right?

On reflection though, we recognised the value of taking a step back. The expert's niche was HR managers and leaders; whilst this is a great niche, the additional value of the course would be to upsell a consultancy concept to the corporate employer and other core products to earn £10,000 – £20,000 per client. A powerful benefit.

Without discussing exactly how a person is moved on in a way they are happy enough to say thank you, we would not have discovered yet another possible product. You see, the secret behind why people are happy to be fired is the work that goes into discovering what the employee really wants to do with their lives. Where there is a poorly performing individual, you will normally find an unhappy person who has lost their passion or drive for their job and are just there because of habit or fear and doubt about moving on. Help them discover what they want to do with their lives and then you have an employee who is happy to change or leave.

Therefore, we realised that using the same expertise, we could build an additional product to help people find their ideal roles and jobs. Perhaps show people how to get their next promotion, or how to identify and apply for roles and jobs that will fulfil them for life.

Originally, this expert's knowledge was just being sold to organisations who wanted to get rid of bad apples, now it can also be positioned to help any employee who is unsuccessful and unhappy because they are in the wrong job. A new, wider and additional market available to them for the simple investment of taking their existing knowledge and designing a new course.

EXPLORE THIRD-PARTY ASSETS

Think about where your expertise and your understanding of your industry are actually being published, and that might give you some clues to spot your value.

If you are posting on Twitter all day with your house renovations, then you will be creating a database (even though it is on Twitter) of people that like and follow you.

Explore your third-party assets:

1. You are creating an online audience, people are following you, you have demonstrated credibility in the world of house renovations on these social media platforms.

2. You have a bank of thought leadership and content on the subject of house renovations that you can revisit/repurpose and use online.

3. Questions to Explore your third-party assets:

    ▶ Do you write about your industry?

    ▶ Do you write lots of articles, news items or trade magazines?

    ▶ Do you write a blog?

    ▶ Do you have a following on social media?

    ▶ How long have you been influencing your industry?

    ▶ What are the major publications in your industry?

    ▶ In which publications or events have you appeared and presented at?

    ▶ Do you have online articles you can use to link to for credibility?

You might just post on Facebook, Instagram and Twitter all the time about your area of expertise. You might be publishing lots of photographs, e.g. house renovations that you've done, or you might be posting lots of photographs of fashion designs that you've made.

EXPLORE AN IDEA & ASSET AUDIT

To help you get clarity on the course target, I have created a spreadsheet tool which draws on everything we have covered in this chapter. It is a tool for you to use in determining whether you have IP that you could sell online and what you might already have that is an asset to your new online product, e.g. existing presentations, videos, books, email lists, social media assets.

This tool will really point you in the right direction of your know-how and IP. It could save you hours and hours of brain fog and clear your way to your online course in a flash. Often, we can't see where the value in our own knowledge is. I have deliberately set out to challenge your thought processes and to try and prompt your subconscious into delivering your best course ideas. Do the audit and then sleep on it and do it again. You will be amazed at what you come up with. It's a little bit magic.

WWW.LORRAINEGANNON.COM/MOREMONEYMOREFUN

You need to write out your areas of opportunity and weigh up the pros and cons.

1. Sit down and complete the spreadsheet of all the areas of potential courses or interests based on your IP. Write out any possible solutions or options you have. Try to get 20 on your list. Sometimes in option number 20 you will find ideas that you may not have done if you weren't pushing to stretch the possibilities and be as creative as possible. Don't move on to number 2 in this list until you have 20 course options.

2. Who is the target customer for your course?

3. What problem are you solving for them?

4. How much content do you have/need? Can you produce a minimum of four hours of content per month?

5. What outcome will your subscriber get from the course?

6. What case studies do you have?

7. Do you have any tools, tricks or smart hacks that you use?

8. Do you have a methodology of how to do something?

9. Do you have your process and system documented?

10. Write out the pros and cons of each idea. Rank the solutions. You can quickly assess each of your 20 course ideas in the spreadsheet tool. If you prefer to do this manually then score each area from 1-20, 20 being the

best idea for each question, and then the next best one scoring 19 and so on and so on. Then review the scores to find the best idea.

Do you have two or three options now that you would want to test?

I hope that writing out your options gives you some clarity on what the best choices for you are. You might want to think about this for a few days. Have a chat with a few customers or potential subscribers and see what they would be interested in.

⌗O
EXPORE
Key Learnings

1. Dig deep and find your passions. Be honest with yourself about your values, interests and skills.

2. Be authentic. Show up with IP that belongs to you and you believe in.

3. Know what problem you can solve. Perhaps you don't think you are solving a problem, but what emotion are you trying to create? Even a craft or art subscription solves a problem. You could be helping people to relax or enjoy the process of creation. How do you make your customer feel?

4. Complete the idea & asset tool at www.lorrainegannon. com/moremoneymorefun

5. You should now have an idea of what your value
    proposition is ready for testing. When you talk about
    your course or subscription, people say "I would buy
    that". There is some interest.

Now you know what you have to offer, you are ready to package it into something to take to potential buyers. The next step is to validate with Expressions of Interest. This will test your IP. The answer to the question "Is my IP worth something?" is really in the hands of the market. Let's find out more...

CHAPTER 12

EXPRESSIONS OF INTEREST

"Do what you have to do,

until you can do what you want to do."

OPRAH WINFREY

WHAT IS EXPRESSIONS OF INTEREST?

The Expressions of Interest stage is about getting real buyers interested in your product. We are now ready to test your idea live in the market. There are so many potential ideas and concepts that I don't even know if they will sell or not, and I don't want to constrain you to the ideas that I've contained in this book. If you feel something is a good idea, then test it and just go for it.

The outcome of the Explore step is you're going to have a value proposition that you can go to market with. You are now going to take Expressions of Interest literally in your product. In other words, we're pre-selling. You won't have a course written; it will not exist. It will still be in your head. The course will exist only if your idea passes the next stage.

This whole step is about taking your idea, then formatting it into a course structure so that you can offer customers an outcome that they are willing to give you money to achieve. If this is successful you can move to the next step to Execute your idea. If you fail, you must go back to Explore.

We teach you to pre-sell your course. This helps our students put their product online and sell quickly. In order to stop overwhelm and procrastination pre-sell your course so that you have paying customers from day one.

WHY IS EXPRESSIONS OF INTEREST IMPORTANT AND WHAT HAPPENS IF YOU DON'T DO IT?

One mistake people make when they write courses is to write the whole course and get to market slowly without really knowing whether anyone is prepared to pay for the product they are spending months creating. We teach you to overcome that by creating an outline first and pre-selling the course before you write the content.

Instead, you are going to take money for the future promise of the course idea. It is important that you take money and convince your customer to pay you for the future delivery of this product. Do not skip this part. The value exchange is the test that your product actually solves a problem for your customers that they are willing to pay for.

Common mistakes when people do this step poorly:

▶ They write a couple of months and start slowly. They lose momentum and only do one or two webinars to pre-sell events.

▶ They write the whole course first without any feedback from their market.

Expressions of Interest: Why people will buy something that doesn't exist

I know you don't believe me, but they will! I can prove over and over how people will buy your idea without it existing. I have done this many times, and it does work if your product has a true value proposition, and if your product doesn't, it's better you know now.

The platform Kickstarter.com has hundreds of examples of people that pay money for the future promise of a product. Normally there is only a graphic or mock-up of the product, a small pitch and then a promise to receive a product later, and perhaps additional benefits depending on the level of funds given.

CASE STUDY
The Power of Pre-sale

On launching an additional product into our business. We used a subject matter expert who gave us the ability to widen our course subjects. Before writing a word of the course we pre-sold 20. Therefore, we had an income of £2k per month before we started. This was a great motivation to write the course. When you know you owe your subscribers a module in 30 days' time, it's amazing how quickly you get to work to write it. It's not just about creating the content but having to do it to a deadline. The power of customers waiting will kill any procrastination you have. You will be off, ready to provide the value you promised.

WHO WANTS TO BUY PRE-LAUNCH?

There are a few reasons why people would engage with you pre-launch of your product:

1. Early adopters

There are a huge bunch of people that like to be the first in every industry. There will always be art collectors looking for the latest talent. There will be people who will buy the latest phone that isn't a high street brand name because it has value to them and solves their problems. They like to be at the cutting edge of developments. The first in the know, the first to own a product.

2. Raving fans

If you are already in business, you will have some customers who are just raving fans. They will buy everything you produce, and you might not be producing enough for them to consume. Give them more to buy and they will buy.

3. They need your product

Yes, unfortunately, people do want you to write your course, they need you to help them solve their problems. *Damn*. You might just have to write this course now.

THE BENEFITS OF GETTING EXPRESSIONS OF INTEREST

1. Validation

You get validation that your product can sell in the market, your sales pitch is working, and you are addressing a need of your customers. It enables you to tweak the content and positioning if you need to. It enables you to test and measure your product and pitch without wasting lots of time creating something that doesn't work.

2. Motivation

I am sure it has crossed your mind that you might get lots of people to buy your course and you will have their money, and then you will have to write the course. Yes? Pre-selling your idea gives you massive motivation. I have launched courses and had 20 subscribers all signed up to pay £100 per month. The potential of earning £2000 per month is a huge motivating factor.

Having 20 subscribers from day one really does mean you have some rocket fuel in your ship to really launch without procrastinating. Without the pre-launch, a lot of you would dither and put off selling the programme until it is finished. If you wait for the whole thing to be completed, you could have missed hundreds of thousands of pounds worth of revenue.

3. Money

You have small amounts of money that you spend on having logos created and buying a few production consumables such as a small microphone, headset or tripod. Be careful to not spend what you cannot refund. If you are at all concerned that you won't be able to deliver your course, you need the ability to refund your customers. Therefore, be careful with your pre-sales money. But yes, you will have some money in the bank from day zero.

4. Time

Your subscribers will wait 4-8 weeks before they expect to see your product. It is good to launch at the beginning of a month. I would normally promise to launch early in the next month or the month after. There is a psychological advantage of starting at the beginning of the month. We all like fresh starts. It's like starting a new diet on a Monday. It also gives your subscribers the chance to get ready; they will often put off starting something new if they are busy or have some obstacle in the way at this moment in time. But ask someone to start in a few weeks' time and most people will often overestimate how much they can achieve in that time and be readier to start at a future date because of that bias. This means you can also buy yourself some time to get going and learn how to write, record and produce your content.

5. Confidence

Expressions of Interest will give you confidence that you are creating something people want and you have a market for. You now should be confident that your IP solves customers' problems.

THE 5 STEPS OF EXPRESSIONS OF INTEREST

Step 1. Write your outline first

Start with an outline of your course content. The outline gives you something to show people and establishes if there is a need or a desire for your course. The outline is an important tool. It's your brochure of what we're going to sell to people at the beginning of your course. Don't write the detail of every single slide and piece of information you're going to give in your course, make it a high level summary. The outline should be in pdf format, held on some kind of landing page or as part of your sales page for your customers to view.

Your outline should cover the monthly deliverables for at least six months but ideally for 12 months. The outline also helps people see the journey they are about to go on with you. It gets them thinking in the way that you are. It helps people see what outcomes they're going to get. They can look through the information and understand some of the content. An outline is often something that people print out. It is one of those things that they actually hold on to as the content of the course.

You want to put something in your programme that's maybe four to five months out that would keep people on the programme because they're anticipating the value that's coming up.

The process of pinning your general idea into a more detailed outline will also give your thinking some format. It's important to keep the outline up to date – a lot of subscribers print it out and use it as an index to follow the course progression. If you change it, mark it up with a revision and also note the refreshed content. This should also be available online so your subscribers can see that you're keeping your course content relevant. This will give the subscriber value and help you write the course each month.

We're going to use the outline to pre-sell the concept to people so that you don't go writing for months and months and months and then find there is no market. We get people subscribed onto your product, which will open at a future date.

These are four slides taken from a PowerPoint presentation, which was used in my online course for this book. It gives the customer confidence that their problem will be sufficiently solved whilst it is sufficiently high level enough for the course content to adapt and change if you need it to. Your customer is essentially assessing the structure of what you will deliver to get to the outcome they want. They essentially don't understand why these things are here, but they trust that your solution has enough structure and content to overcome their problems.

MODULE 1

MODULE	WHAT'S INCLUDED
INTRODUCTION	How the course works. How to reach out to me.
• **Mindset**	Set yourself up well. The difference between successful students and unsuccessful.
• **Goal setting**	What are the right goals?
• **Start well**	How you start is important to overall success.
• **What do I really need?**	Truths around starting small and how you don't need a massive list.
• **My Beliefs**	What are you saying to yourself, that could be sabotaging your success?
• **Impact & Money**	The more money you earn the greater the success and impact you can have. Reset your money mindset.

MODULE 2

MODULE	WHAT'S INCLUDED
WHY ONLINE COURSES?	
• **Time for money trap**	What is the time for money trap? How value can replace your time.
• **Recurring income**	What is recurring income and what are its qualities?

MODULE	WHAT'S INCLUDED
• **Online courses why they work**	How the modern world of online education is taking off.
• **Future of learning**	Why education needs a disruption and where will education go in the future.
• **Right time right place– Start now**	Obstacles and how to avoid them.
• **Time to profit**	You know more than you think you do. Other people need your help. Teach and help them to earn profit.

MODULE 3

MODULE	WHAT'S INCLUDED
THE 3 PILLARS OF ONLINE COURSES	
• **- Pillar 1 USP & IP**	What do you know that can help others?
• **- Pillar 2 Structure**	How do you create a recurring income from your know-how?
• **- Pillar 3 Sales**	Can you sell your know how?

MODULE 4

MODULE	WHAT'S INCLUDED
THE 5 E'S	
• **The 5 Es Method**	The 5 Es journey and how this is designed to get quick results in 5 easy steps.
• **Explore**	How to find what you know, that could be an online course
• **Expressions of Interest**	How to find out if the market wants your products.
• **Execute**	How to create the product.
• **Engage**	How to keep your customers.
• **Extend**	How to grow your product and extend the numbers of members and subscribers.

Step 2. Break your subject into five areas

It's like looking in at the beginning of this book and seeing an index and table of contents. You can kind of get a feel for the content in the book and what's going to occur and happen and the structure the author's using. It's the same with a course. As the author of the course, you're going to demonstrate to individuals what the backbone and the skeleton of your course is. This will be the basis of your methodology to start with. A methodology is powerful. It gives your product IP of its very own. I have the 5 Es methodology to get your knowledge online, so you know that I have a process which works.

I've asked you to spread the content over 6-12 months and now I have said spread your subject into five areas.

There are several ways to manage this:

1. Each month cover a small section of each of the five areas, gradually building in depth.

2. Have a basics month, a summary month and then spend two months on each area. This is powerful to get people to your last month. It may also be quite natural because the subject is progressive.

3. Have a basics and advanced section of each of the five areas, which will give you a minimum of 10 units. Ideally, try and get to 12 units.

Step 3. Build a landing page

A landing page is a specific place where you warm up a lead or you might take them to a specific offer and tell them more about that offer. The objective of a landing page is to take you to one place to get you to buy something or give your email address or phone number in exchange for getting something valuable.

A landing page is very specific, and it has a one to one action, whereas a website and a homepage would have many actions that you can take. The difference between a home page and a landing page is a homepage is on a website, which has multiple pages and links built behind it. There are lots of different pages and typically a homepage can have maybe 30, 40, sometimes 60 different links to different places in the website home. The problem with that is that your customer is going to be taken all over the place and can go off and explore and just generally engage in your website, who you are, what your purpose is, etc. They check out your pictures, what your values are, why you're in business and why you're doing what you're doing.

The most valuable thing you can get from a landing page is an email address; out and out, they are the most cost-efficient lead generating activity that you can do.

People tend to be more reluctant to give telephone numbers. They don't want to talk to that many people. They tend to see that as very personal and private information. If you are taking telephone numbers, you might want to tell the prospect why and what context because they typically don't want to give you that kind of information.

If you are going to sell your product, you need a landing page and payment process to complete the Expressions of Interest part of launching your course. A landing page is a single web page that acts like a brochure. By the time the customer has read through it all, they should be very keen to buy.

As digital entrepreneurs, we will create an online brochure that actually sells your product in the form of a landing page. Your brochure has details on all of the features, benefits, ideas, key problems and key solutions that you are delivering.

There are many landing page providers and platforms that you can use to build your page WWW.LEADPAGES.COM or WWW.WIX.COM or WWW.KAJABI.COM all have templates you can use. You do not need to create a full website until you have got some Expressions of Interest. Your landing page could be quite simple. If you are going to get people to sign up, you need a process to go through. You just need a few bits of information that builds trust.

Basic model for landing page copy

▶   Who is this for?

▶   What problem are you solving?

▶   Why us? (include social proof)

▶   Why this works for them?

▶   Why now?

If you'd like to see a landing page in action then head over to WWW.LORRAINEGANNON.COM/MOREMONEYMOREFUN If you register on there you should see the landing page copy and the kinds of follow-up information I provide you. Please copy the general principles of my page.

Other elements you need on your landing page

▶ The special pre-sale price (see below for info on pricing).

▶ Confirm the payment terms, e.g. cancel any time, £9.99 for the first month and then £x per month thereafter, and any terms and conditions.

▶ Your privacy policy – what you will do with the person's data, especially in light of GDPR.

▶ Payment processing – I would advise you to use a payment portal like PayPal or Stripe to take the first payment.

▶ If you are going to use one of the E-Learning platforms like https://kajabi.com then this is all built into the system. You can even use a FREE trial to get you going.

Video on your landing page

Google found that video is watched to gain awareness online. We've seen the most growth recently and 70% of business to business buyers are now watching videos throughout their path to purchase.

What price to put on your landing page

Pricing is the most emotive part of an online course. It is where you part with your intellectual property and your knowledge, but you won't get the high value one to one consultation fees. A part of you will feel like you are giving away the world, and on the other hand, you will feel slightly embarrassed to charge anything too high. It's a balancing act – the higher the price, the more likely you will have high churn and the bigger the decision to start the course in the first place. Some of our products are £250 per month plus VAT. Our product has the potential to change people's lives, give them freedom and financial security for the rest of their lives. We help entrepreneurs change their lives with property.

Pricing and course type

If your course can help people earn more money, then you can charge a lot for it. You want to be looking at the extra earning power you've given your customers over two to three years' worth of value and dividing that by 10. Most people would be looking for 10 times their investment growth for the money they pay you for your course.

A hobby course is different. If you have a hobby or a community membership, you might need to price it a little bit lower, but you might get more members because the entry price is quite low. You're providing valuable information for people.

If you have a preventative cost course (one that helps people avoid problems or costs), you might want to look at how much money you'll be saving people by enrolling in your course. Think through how you might be helping your subscribers, but also the costs you might be preventing them from incurring, which would add value to your membership, which means you can charge more for it. How much are your subscribers' problems hurting them? People are more motivated to move away from something that is causing them pain than move towards something that would give them pleasure.

Self-development courses, e.g. reducing anxiety, are hugely valuable as health is a very important aspect of people's lives, and without health we don't really have much else. Pricing is an area you need to test and measure.

Early bird prices

As you launch a new product you will be offering an early adopters price promotion. Always communicate the deadline for your early adopters price. This creates urgency and scarcity; you can open and close offers or you can choose to do multiple offers.

The power of 99

We are all looking for a solution at a price we can afford. However, we will spend whatever it costs to get a solution we really value. A price that's £100 is a three-digit number, but something like £99 is a two-digit number. Why do most retailers prefer a £99 price point to £100. It's not because they have lots of £1 coins to get rid of. How does that price look when someone is buying? Bigger? If you're going to advertise at £99 or £100 then I would suggest £99 will work better because the number seems smaller to most people who are making a buying decision.

No round numbers

Another consideration is that round numbers don't work very well. They often infer that there's no thought process and a pricing level has just been set arbitrarily. If two products are worth roughly £50, one that's £47.25 seems more thought out than the one that's £50. Your pricing can demonstrate value to your customer.

Bonuses and deals

It's nice to offer bonuses to certain groups of people, e.g. webinar attendees to encourage people to buy there and then. Remember, we want to encourage people to take action. However, you do not give away so much that you can't deliver on it. You don't want to be creating yourself more work on a one to one basis, but there's nothing wrong with perhaps arranging a group coaching call to support a great start. This could be a lot of work if you are not careful, you could limit the calls to the first 20 customers.

The other part of offering bonuses is you want to set something that lasts past a trial period. You want to stop that whole, "I'm going to cancel a week later", and actually offer people bonuses that occur in the next month or so, and further out in the course. These are bonuses that you keep to yourself, but typically bonuses that you offer as a one-off surprise element, after signing up. This will give you huge credibility and give your customers a remarkable experience.

Step 4. Send people to your landing page

Now you need to get people to your brilliant landing page and that requires a funnel.

What is a funnel?

A funnel is a way of understanding and following the customer journey from start (not knowing about you or your product at all) to finish (spending their money with you). There are various stages, which I'll outline below, these form a sequence:

DIAGRAM: A FUNNEL & FILTERING OF TARGETED POTENTIAL CUSTOMERS INTO PROSPECTS AND THEN INTO CUSTOMERS.

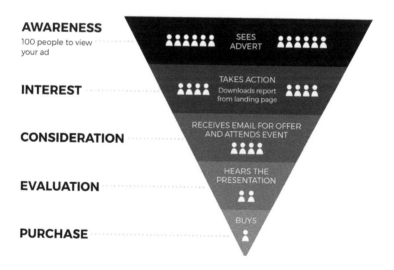

AWARENESS
100 people to view your ad — SEES ADVERT

INTEREST — TAKES ACTION
Downloads report from landing page

CONSIDERATION — RECEIVES EMAIL FOR OFFER AND ATTENDS EVENT

EVALUATION — HEARS THE PRESENTATION

PURCHASE — BUYS

"

The percentage of the people aware of your product that actually buy is called the conversion rate.

"

1. **Awareness**. This is when your potential customers first find out about you/your product, e.g. when they first see an advert. They know you exist.

2. **Interest**. This is when the potential customer (prospect) has got sufficiently interested to take some sort of action, e.g. click a link to your website or download some of your content. The prospect may not have spent any time or money on your business at this point. They may have scanned an ad and an email for 30 seconds.

3. **Consideration**. This is when the prospect spends time and/or money considering your offers and products, e.g. the prospect may have bought a book or listened to a few podcast episodes for a few hours.

4. **Purchase**. Now they are ready and willing to buy your product or service.

Selling online and online courses, or any subscription, is all about having a funnel like that in the diagram above. It's about taking your potential customers on the whole journey from the start of your process to actually buying from you. You will need to make them aware of you, then get them to engage with your content to eventually become customers.

If you think of a big audience and you are trying to get a small section to come over to your stall and buy something, those that buy from you have converted from a prospect (they had the potential to become a sale) into a sale.

The percentage of the people aware of your product that actually buy is called the conversion rate.

It is just common sense that not everyone that sees you advert will buy from you; conversion rates are always going to be less than 100%. This process is called funnelling because you start with a really wide top at the start of the process and you are channelling prospects through a process to drop out of the bottom as a sale.

LEADS & DEALS MANAGEMENT

Depending on what market you are in, you will see some slight variations. But I find a good rule of thumb that is broadly applicable across all industries is the following statistics from research and my own confirmed experience.

79% of marketing leads never convert into sales[16].

35-50% of sales go to the vendor that responds first[17].

This is a benchmark report of conversion rates. Broadly, it applies across all markets but was tested on business to business marketing. Your niche may have differences, but this is a good benchmark to refer to.

DIAGRAM: ENQUIRIES THAT BECOME LEADS

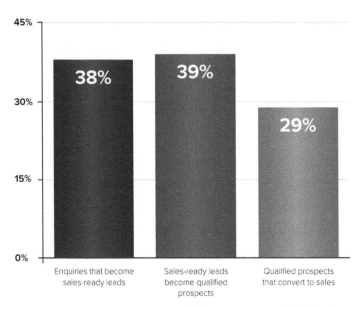

Source: MarketingSherpa B2B Marketing Benchmark Survey 2009. Methodology Fielded April 15-20, 2009, N=1,147

Breakdown of these percentages applied to 100 Enquiries.

100	Enquiries
38	Sales Ready
14	Qualified Prospects
4	Convert to Sales

Boost your conversion rate

Previously, in old marketing strategies for newspapers and TV, a very broad advert perhaps would have gone into a newspaper which may have been relevant to some of the readers and completely irrelevant to others. We can now use modern technology to target only people our ad will be relevant to. I'm not a technology geek, but I am a very process driven and return on investment focused person. I love working in funnel metrics. Your funnel will allow you to follow a process, deliver and record your information at each level, enabling you to scale the selling of your online courses.

We now have the ability to niche, to target people based on specific interests, thanks to the amazing powers and the data collection of some of these software platforms. Facebook is an amazing database; in effect, it tracks your social and entertainment values alongside your business values in a very predictable way. We can clearly see what our customers' values are and then reach out to them with targeted campaigns and adverts.

Have a webinar

Webinars are events on the theme of your course and can provide the perfect opportunity to get people into your funnel. You can sell to your audience and give a special offer that is only valid on the day of the webinar.

A webinar is a live stream of a video presentation. You write slides (on PowerPoint or keynote) and then present them live over the internet using software like GoToWebinar. It is best to practise this first before you do a live webinar. You invite people to your webinar via a link that you can email them or share on social media.

What is the difference between a live and evergreen webinar?

Some webinar platforms will host pre-recorded material at set times; this is called an evergreen webinar. The advantages of evergreen webinars are:

- ▶ Automated.

- ▶ It doesn't take your time every week to host live.

- ▶ Your prospects can access it at their convenience.

- ▶ A good webinar can be repeated effortlessly; your performance won't change with your current mood or energy levels.

However, I find that live webinars perform better. Live environments always perform better because you can tailor your message, you can speak to your customers, and you can answer their questions in that live environment. You can use their first names in the software, much more powerful than having an evergreen webinar.

You can comment on topical events and recent news. Your prospect gets a sense that you are there.

But to keep this sustainable, what we do is test and measure with some live webinars and when we find a webinar that converts successfully, it is then put into an evergreen format. And then we will ramp up the system and traffic to the landing pages, e.g. through ads, to get more email addresses and then to send more people to our webinar. This helps remove our time and puts the sales process into a more automated funnel. But as you'd expect, all the effort is upfront.

What should you include in your webinar?

A webinar should have an outline as follows:

1. Why You? Your expertise/authority to speak on the subject.

2. Why Them? Pick case studies that your customer can relate to.

3. Why This? Content of your course.

4. How they will achieve the results.

5. Course outline.

6. Course structure and format – what you need to do, how often content is released.

7. Why Now? Your offer. Why should I buy now? What are you offering for me to make the decision now?

A webinar format is basically a slide deck, a PowerPoint, a presentation. We talk to our customers and we explain why they should work with you. Why them? Why are we talking to them? What is their problem? What is our solution? Then our discussion flows as follows:

- **Why us?**

Why are we entitled to give them the course information? Why are we entitled to talk to them about this product? What are our qualifications? What success have we had? Depending on your course this could vary greatly, e.g. what grade piano did you pass? How famous are you, or where have you played and what kind of art exhibitions have you been in? What photography awards have you won? Obviously all relevant to the course subject. What gives you the entitlement to talk to these people? Don't forget there might be some successes from your existing clients, and you may want to include these case studies in your webinar.

- **Why them?**

You need your customer to identify their problems, as already discussed. What are the problems your target customer needs to solve? Therefore, when you are considering why your customer should buy from you, make sure to include details about the problems they have, what your alternative is, and why what they are doing now will not work for them. Will their problems get worse?

- **Why this?**

Then you talk to a customer about why this product. Why do they need this product in their life? Why can't they just go onto Google and get the information you can provide? Google is a historic review of past published content. There's no course progression. YouTube is one of those places where you go to learn how to make slime for your kids. Or you might go in and you might learn how to fix your tumble dryer or how to change a wheel, but it's fairly instant results. Why does your product work? Tell the story of your success and how this is included in your product.

This is why your customers would be using online courses. Your customers need you and your online courses. Because Google becomes outdated. If you're in a technology environment or you're teaching people about business skills. How much has changed in the last three years? And how much will change in the next two?

Technology is changing the pace of the world and your customers. They should be listening to your up to date, relevant, thought leader learning. This is why they should be with you.

- **How they will achieve the results**

You will need to explain exactly how you discovered your solution to make it really credible. Why/how did you recognise this solution that you are proposing to them? Did you need their same problem solving? Have you spent years trying various things before you perfected the solution? Can they learn from your experiments and mistakes? Can you save them time? You can provide case studies and information about why the product works. How will your product guide them?

- **Course outline**

I shared an example of a course outline earlier in this chapter. The course outline can be a simple table of contents. Buyers are not going to be interested unless they know what they can expect from you, what you will be covering and when. An outline gives them confidence that you will comprehensively cover the subject (i.e. comprehensively solve their problem) and have planned your content for the future months. The visual of an outline is powerful because it helps people see that your course actually exists.

- **Course structure and format**

You will obviously need to explain to people what they are committing to (how many months) and take an initial payment. If you are taking ongoing payments forever or for the next 12 months, then your customers will need to understand their commitment.

You also need to communicate the course launch date, take email addresses and then have a mechanism to let people access your course when it is ready (most systems have a way of opening the course and releasing content on set dates).

I use PayPal to take an initial payment because it's easy, familiar and we get the email addresses and funds, then the customer is just waiting for the product.

- **Why now?**

You're going to want to give your customers a reason to do this now. There might be a special offer or there might be some information or content that's particularly relevant to their business at the moment. At the end of your one-off webinar, you need to offer to your clients what they're going to buy. You need to give them all the information about the course content, the outline, and the link to go to purchase the offer today. It is a good idea to make it time bound; this motivates people to take action. How often have you thought about buying something, but then, as time goes by, you forget about why you need it? And then you don't take action.

Time kills sales unfortunately, so you need a call to action and offer for your subscribers to take from the webinar. You do want to help people make a decision there and then. There's nothing unethical about this. This is just simply how the human brain works. If you really believe in your product, you're giving people an opportunity to change their lives or improve something or even get passionate about new skills, so why shouldn't you help them make that decision? Once you sell your offer to people, you want to have an email to follow-up and make sure that your customers can get something from you that confirms their purchase. You'd be surprised by how many people think they have been scammed without some sort of follow-up confirmatory email. Don't underestimate the value of actually starting straightaway, now. People want to consume instantly nowadays, so they'll want to get stuck in. If you have any instructions or some starting up advice, email it across to your customers.

Get on social media

The best thing about social media is that most people don't use it with a business purpose, they consume content for their own personal entertainment. You're much more likely to stand out if you sit down and work out a formulaic approach to social media. How are you going to get online?

Social media is free, but for a few pounds a day you can boost posts and get great views and audience engagement. You can even tailor what your audience behaviours are and their interests you want to target. Don't set up a Facebook business page and post there all day long without spending money on boosting your post to an audience or no one will see your content. Facebook stopped promoting businesses for free a long time ago. Things like pay per click adverts on social media are really cheap and you can get quite a lot of awareness and boosting of your profile with a few pounds a week.

Which social media platforms should you try?

Firstly, it's a good idea to investigate your competitors. Just see what they're doing, what they're up to, and see if you can understand if you should niche or change your format. Then look at your customer demographics and think where they might be hanging out and try to spend as much time as possible on there. Then scan for key phrases, words and hashtags on social media to understand where your customers are hanging out and what they are talking about.

The social media platforms:

Facebook has a more chatty feature with lots of text and some video.

Instagram has lots more image-related content and tends to be a more positive environment with less "tit for tat" commenting. It is very good for things like visual photos if you have a product that is art or photography or some kind of modelling or makeup, etc. Instagram has a lot of motivational posts. This can be harnessed by you as an educator and course providers to show how much your customers can improve their lives. Instagram is experiencing massive growth, and you should be there to get in on the action.

Twitter is more on demand news generated content, very popular with the media and journalists. You must hang out on Twitter to be attracting the attention of the media.

LinkedIn is great for business to business and it has a much more professional feel to it, and you are less likely to see pictures of people's dinners and family photos.

YouTube is a great way to get a big following; it requires consistent and prolific content generation.

Try to focus on one platform and dominate it first. Then switch to a second. You'll be surprised by how focusing on one platform harnesses results in another.

What to say on social media

Remember you can connect to up to 20,000 others on LinkedIn and you can have 5000 friends on your own personal Facebook. Find where your audience are and go and connect and friend as many people as you can. Then start posting free tips and advice to help them. Build engagement with your posts, like other people's posts, comment sympathetically and give others the validation they seek. Comment in other people's groups; don't advertise but contribute. It is worth checking the group rules because you may well be able to advertise freely.

Ask questions on your posts. Tell everybody what you are creating online. Build up interest and ask people to just say they are interested in a post. No other commitment, this will build your social proof. You are asking people to give zero commitment, but it starts to build credibility and the social proof that you have an interesting product. This will help your business all round.

Start building your list

You may already have an audience in an existing business database. Use it. Sell to it. You need to build your emailing list because we've learnt that emails and having your own data is going to sell your product for you much easier than selling direct from social media. Once you've got somebody's email address, you've got their attention, and you're not competing with other tweets, other Facebook posts and all the other videos on the social media networks. You need your own data.

We discuss this a lot more in later chapters because it is an ongoing requirement, but you need to be consistently building a list to sell to.

I want you to start emailing your list. We're looking to give something away for free in return for an email address, we call that a lead magnet. What information do people want? They might want some white papers, e.g. seven ideas or tools that help solve their problem or share what high performers do in their industry. Outline a success story and the key take-aways.

Step 5. Make sales (launch offer & payment)

Launch offer price

You'll need a launch offer. Launch your programme at such a low value and offer a lifetime price that people would be crazy not to buy. It also gives you some money to play with at the start. It's not uncommon for us to sell 20 to 30 sub-scriptions on a programme without even having the content written.

When you're pricing your products, you can also charge a smaller fee for month 1. Typically, we start month 1 at £9.99. That initial payment is to cover the cost of the customer acqui-sition (anything we might have to spend to get them into our funnel, like Facebook ads). It contributes to the customer costs, but also makes the subscribers value their purchase; it's not free and without value. Free can be bad, and it also means you will get some false sales.

Trials

A trial is a no commitment short period of time. It doesn't require anyone to sign up past 28 days, but it's a nice way to build trust and get people into the product. A trial typically has an initial lower price than the whole programme. A new customer can come onto a trial with us and we normally take the barriers of entry right down to £9.99 as the initial fee; I've also seen $1 trials. The first thing that this does is it makes people think about what payment card or bank account they are going to use. It's the signal that they've got to go and get their credit card out.

A free trial without an initial payment can kill sales because people who weren't expecting to put their card details in suddenly have to put their card details in for £0. They weren't expecting that. If they have to pay £1, they immediately know they are going to be asked for a small fee. On our E-Learning platform we always take payment details. This will stop some people from purchasing, but it does mean that serious people have to consider that they are going to get charged in a few months' time, unless they cancel.

A trial that doesn't take card details or an initial payment is not a sale. You've just thrown your hard work in selling someone on the concept of your product into confusion. They have no reason to value your product. You've not given them the chance to exchange their money for your value. The conversion is being pushed into the future (when they may pay for it at a later date), which creates apathy in terms of actually working with the product. The equation is unbalanced, your prospect will drift off to another product, overwhelmed and confused that you haven't taken them on as a customer. Some people want to buy, let them buy.

EXPRESSIONS OF INTEREST
Key Learnings

1. Some of the key learnings in this section have been about finding out who might want to buy your course and who would be interested.

2. A lot of people will buy and pre-pay for something that doesn't actually exist already.

3. We're also going to write our outline first. The outline is very important, it gives the subscriber the structure, and it also gives you something to work with. It's a sales tool at this point in time.

4. The structure is actually on a monthly basis so that you get your monthly recurring income off the back of your course.

5. Have you completed the idea & asset spreadsheet?

6. What content have you already got?

7. What can you repurpose?

8. Do you have some content that's published?

9. Do you have some videos, or other handouts that you can repurpose and use for your course outline?

10. Create a landing page and checkout process.

11. Run a webinar or a live event. You can bring people into a classroom, a strategy session, it could be a course. Email your list. Message your connections. Post an announcement on social media.

12. Launch your product and get lots of Expressions of Interest.

Hopefully, you'll get lots of Expressions of Interest. If not, then don't be disheartened, this is where you need to go back to the Explore cycle.

We want to come out of this section with some Expressions of Interest, and it's not uncommon to get up to 30 Expressions of Interest from four webinars over a month with a list of 500 emails. But if you've got a fairly small list, then be happy to get a few.

Don't be afraid to repeat this process either.

CHAPTER 13

EXECUTE

"Do or do not, there is no try."

YODA, STAR WARS

WHAT IS EXECUTE?

Execute is the stage where you actually produce and design the course platform!

You will produce your course a month at a time. As you sell your course, you write a month, a month is released and then you sell the next month. Your membership grows steadily, you earn money and sell more subscriptions and then after 12 months, you can sell the whole programme if you want to or write another course, or if you have an infinite course subject then you carry on.

You've established the outline and the content of your course. You should have written the outline by now and be ready to actually deliver this to your customers and your prospects. Now you need to go into the detail. You need to really plan so you've got enough content to last a good 9 – 12 months. Don't forget to break it down into the first section of quick wins or foundation building. Quick wins help people to get engaging in your programme, and you might want to look at 6 to 10 weeks' worth of actions and tips to get people started. Then you're going to go into greater depth on certain subjects, and then you're going to give additional content and additional values in your course. That forms the outline of your courses. You want to be sure that you've got at least the titles and the headings already set up and planned out. Remember to include your methodology.

WHY IS EXECUTE IMPORTANT AND WHAT HAPPENS IF YOU DON'T DO IT?

I am sorry to say that if you create something of value and people sign up and buy it before it launches then you will need to actually create the product otherwise you will have to refund the money. But that's good, yes?

The Execute part here is important and that is obvious, but don't rush it. Do it with quality, time and well thought out and designed content. That way, you will create an asset that serves you for many years. This methodology is deliberately designed to give you momentum to write and momentum to create your products.

Nothing is harder than trying to complete something that you don't know will sell. So now your customers are paid up and waiting, you have to deliver.

▶ **Deadlines.** These are very important because you've made a commitment to your prospects and customers that you are going to deliver your online course on time. It's important that you keep that commitment. Otherwise, your customers' trust levels go down and they may end their subscription early. You also need to do what you said you were going to do. If you've committed to releasing the

"

Nothing is harder than trying to complete something that you don't know will sell. So now your customers are paid up and waiting, you have to deliver.

"

▶ content at a certain point in the month, then you ought to honour that commitment. Otherwise, your customers and subscribers will have a good reason to demand a refund, and we don't want lots of refunds. People are waiting for your content. They will wait, but they won't want to be waiting and they will only wait until the expected date.

If your content is not there, it's late and you haven't delivered, then you can expect people to get disenchanted and stop engaging in your course. Keeping engagement high is a really important factor of your online course.

▶ **Motivation.** You need to record your content and Execute your product professionally and properly so that you don't become embarrassed by it. It's important for you to feel proud of your product, because when you feel proud of it, your mindset changes and you will sell it more successfully. You will believe in it. You'll be able to transfer that energy and that value, and more people will buy into your product. You want to make sure that you believe in the success of this product as you will transfer that to your customers. Make sure that you're doing things professionally; people will be listening and watching your content.

▶ **Methodology and Product.** If you don't have the right motivation to Execute your product, your brain and your thought processes become confused. That means the methodology and the product itself will lack clarity and it will become confusing to the consumer. Try and keep your motivation high. Your course needs to be professional so that you and your consumer are motivated to complete the product.

▶ **Time management.** You want to make sure that you're not in a rush and you want to pace out and think about the content you want in your modules. You need to have thought about your processes, your methodology and your core messages and outcomes. If you don't do this properly, then basically you know you're going to miss your deadlines, your motivation is going to go down and the time management of the whole programme is going to be unsuccessful and it's going to fail. And what happens is people start asking for refunds. They start bugging you about when the content is going to be released. People will wait a few days, but if you promised something would launch on the 1st of a month and you are more than a few days late, they will challenge you for refunds. That puts more pressure on you and the whole thing becomes a whole lot less fun. Keep in mind your deadlines, make sure you can deliver.

CASE STUDY
USE THE RIGHT PLATFORM

I know a man that is very good at designing websites and he uses WordPress plugin to host his courses. It makes sense that if you have that skill you would use it to get the cheapest platforms and software. However, the WordPress plugins break. Every time the system updated some of the code didn't work as it did, and then the course content didn't sync, and the students lost their content and demanded refunds. It only takes one payment a month to break even on most learning management systems (LMS) content platforms. Use software that makes your life easy. You need to be selling your product, not coding or dealing with stressful technical glitches. Some people use solutions that only meet half their needs, often to save costs, but ultimately it can cost you even more when your unhappy customers want their money back. I worked for a large multinational company that spent millions on a computer system that did everything from manage production processes to purchase ledger, debt collection, stock control, payroll, management accounts, everything. It was amazing. The quality of data was unrivalled, the clarity of knowing that all the data was in one place. I am definitely an advocate of having an end to end process that sits in one platform.

For me, this book is about actually giving you the confidence and the understanding of how to market yourself as a course provider. I could quite easily write the book on how to use multiple different platforms and the pros and cons of each one. Personally, I don't think it matters which one you use as long as you move on and develop your course and publish it; so given there are lots of different platforms out there, the one thing that you do need to do is start.

THE 5 STEPS OF EXECUTE

You follow my 5 step process on production:

1. Product brand

2. Content design

3. Presenting

4. Product creation/production

5. Tools and outsourcing

Step 1. Product brand

Think about the name that you could give to your product that gives it an identity and clearly speaks to the right audience. It's a package. Something of value has a name and values we associate with them. For example, what products do you think of when I say "Apple"? The iPhone, the iPad, etc.

Plan the modules and methodologies, use alliteration, the seven Ls, or the six Ps, or the five Es (as I'm using here). You need that kind of alliteration. It helps people remember things.

Give your product a name. It brings it to life and gives it an identity. Rolex names all of its watches. You have the GMT Master, the Date Just, the Sub-Mariner, etc. Each of these names convey values and emotions. If your customers refer to your products by name, this will deliver a huge brand boost to your products. It creates conversations around the product, and not just you and your business.

You can also use mnemonics (these spell something out). For example, if you were running a photography course you could structure it so that each letter in "photo" spells one of your modules, e.g. P could be "Portraits", etc. I would use a thesaurus; see if you can align some of the names of your methodologies to a relevant term. It also gives you some unique IP. Your subscriber can then see that what you're doing has been thought out and is structured. People like structure when they're learning. You may do this in the outline, but you may not have drilled deep enough to develop this methodology. If you haven't, then now, in Execute, is the time to perfect this naming, process and methodology.

Step 2. Content design

What they want/need

What mistakes do your customers make, and what solutions do you have in place that you could communicate to your customers to help them buy your product? What a customer wants and what a customer needs are sometimes two very different things.

We always try to give customers their wants as well as their needs.

Sometimes the needs are a little bit boring, e.g. a property training product. Not a lot of people want to hear about licensing and the detail behind compliance of licensing in properties. It's hard work but it's essential to make sure they make the right investment, but actually what they do want to do is the fun colour choosing interior design and pattern choices. The interior design does add value and does add revenue, but essentially, what colour the walls are is not important to the overall concept of owning and running a house. But it is the part of the journey the customer enjoys the most.

Do think about what you want in your product that is a "nice to have" as opposed to an "essential", because you're looking to create remarkable products and delighted customers through your customers' journey.

Bite-sized is best

Each module of your course needs to be broken down into bite-sized lessons. There is a reason why your school lessons were never eight hours long! It's too much to take in. Attention spans are actually very short, particularly if your audience is older people who have left school years ago; they have a very short attention span and very busy lives. You want your students to be successful, so you need to give them all the opportunities you can to be successful.

By giving them some of the basic information and then perhaps repeating it later and going into greater depth, you will find that your customer retention or churn rates will be better than if you just simply gave all the content in one go.

Build in breaks

Don't be afraid to ask questions and ask people to pause or stop their learning at any point in time. Although we will be recording videos and audio files, you can ask people to stop the video and the audio file and reflect on their learnings of your course. What this does is it helps people think through and create value in their brain against the questions you've asked.

Provide success tools

We provide people with success tools. These can be Excel spreadsheets that are pre-populated with information or formula. People love these kinds of tools. Very often what they sign up for is to get access to these types of tools and processes that you've invented/created.

You can also provide a course handout in Word or PDF, what we would call a "downloadable". A "downloadable" is valuable to your customers because they can print it and stick it on the wall. It keeps them focused and engaged and reminds them to complete the course so they keep revisiting the product on a regular basis.

Juicy extras

If you are charging enough, you could throw in a group live call with Skype or Zoom. Agree to answer emails. Manage the potential time it will take you by grouping activities up and do multi-coaching. A lot of your subscribers will have the same challenges and when one person raises an issue it will also help others.

Repeat yourself

Giving them some of the basic information and then perhaps repeating it later and going into greater depth, you will find that your customer retention or churn rates will be better than if you just simply gave all the content in one go.

"Repetition is the mother of learning, the father of action, which makes it the architect of accomplishment."

ZIG ZIGLAR

Repetition is not a bad thing. The Ebbinghaus curve is a curve where we map time with the retention of information and the number of times the information is recalled and repeated. You should include a certain amount of repetition in your content for your subscribers to learn.

DIAGRAM: RATE OF FORGETTING WITH STUDY/REPETITION

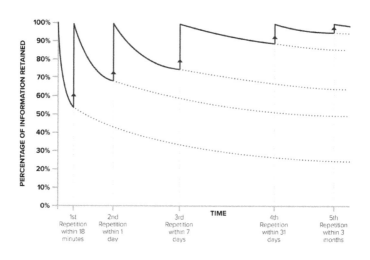

The retention and recall of information lasts a lot longer the more times it is repeated. After the fourth repetition of data, retention typically stays above 90% and remains there. The first repetition of information has to be quite soon after the learning. The retention rate can drop to a staggering 55%, which is very low. Therefore, summarising and keeping your modules to 15 minutes is great for learning. And this is where online courses win over live events, because typically people come away and, two to three days later, they've forgotten half of the content. An online course means you can repeat and summarise, which is a very effective way of learning for your customers. Build some repetition and deeper explorations of content into your course outline too, to capture this benefit naturally.

One of the messages you want to give out to subscribers is to just go into your core programme every day, for 5 to 10 minutes, and either revisit something or learn something every day to keep their engagement high.

Step 3. Presenting

A lot of people have a fear of public speaking. This can translate into the world of presenting in webinars, or actually running a live event in a classroom. If you do, there are a few tactics that can help:

1. Think about how you would present yourself and visualise yourself doing that.

2. Try to remember that you've got a lot of expertise and value to offer people; you know your stuff.

3. Fake it till you make it. Be confident, try and present your best self. Try to put the scared, fearful person behind you and try to draw out the confident person that's inside.

4. Practice. Keep practising; perhaps record a few dummies where you don't have an audience. Go through and

record yourself and listen back. You'll be surprised at how good you'll think you are. Live recordings are easier than pre-recorded. Live is authentic; your brain takes over and makes it work.

5. When you're writing your slides and your presentation notes, put in the PowerPoint presentation or in the keynotes at the bottom of your slides, the notes and the little antidotes that you want to get across to your audience. This will really help you when you dry up, or perhaps don't know what to say next.

6. Tell stories. We're all pre-programed to listen and also tell stories. Since we've been children, we've all had stories told to us. This will really help you get into your flow.

7. Relax, people prefer the natural you. So what if the dog barks in the background? Obviously, if you've got to get up and answer the door to the postman, then this might not be ideal, but actually does it really matter? Does it really detract from the quality of the presentation? It's better to get something out there and be prolific rather than perfect.

Step 4. Product creation/production

Building your content

Plan your modules, your process and know your customers' outcome.

Summarise your content for your customers and your new subscriber.

Reinforce the learnings, what key outcomes you're trying to get people to.

You've got 15 minutes, break that down into chunks, e.g. you'll have a couple of minutes of intro and the main content and then a couple of minutes of summarising at the end. Use that to work out how long you have for each of your main content points. You don't need to script the whole thing, but I think it's useful to have an outline, and some notes.

Remember that if you summarise within the first 18 minutes of teaching somebody something new, then actually the learning goes up from the Ebbinghaus curve.

Kit

You need to work out if you're recording via a small smartphone or whether you're going to buy a video camera. If you are buying something a bit more heavy duty, bear in mind it will create bigger files, which will require more storage space and computer power, and it'll take you longer to edit, simply from the size of higher quality video files.

You want to think about what sort of sound quality you're going to produce. Do make sure you have a good quality microphone. We've experimented with many in the past. If you're spending about £50 or more on a microphone, then you've probably got something that is good quality. Any less than that and you tend to end up with something that has a lot of buzzing and noise in the background. Always listen back to your recordings through plugged in headphones and not through the computer audio. The quality is different. Don't forget, you want people to listen to your course and be successful at it, so provide great audio quality where you can.

You need decent lighting. If you're going to present in front of a camera, you need to make sure that you've got the video camera set up on a tripod, so that you can actually see what's going on. If you are going to record outside, you need to think about the sound and how wind will be picked up on the mic.

It's also important to think about the backdrop (a backdrop is what is behind you when you are recording). Will it be corporate colours, or any other background that is relevant to your subject? You can get backdrops off Amazon.

If all this really challenges you technically, and there is a danger you will do nothing, super simple solution – record a video on a tripod with your smartphone. You can buy microphones that plug into a phone. Put it on a tripod and stand in front of it with a clipboard and record. Then load that up into your platform.

Recording content

Try to do your recording in one take and not worry too much about ums, ahs and going wrong. You want to be as professional as you can as quickly as you can. Remember, the more that you do this, the easier it is.

You might want to stack some of the content, so that you can record three or four modules all in one go. To produce and edit your videos you can use simple editing tools on iPhone, or you can get editing software that will just enable you to cut out bits that you're not happy with.

There are two main ways to record content:

1. **Presenting and narrating a screen capture**

2. **In front of a camera**

Screen capture

This is where you write up a presentation on PowerPoint, and then you talk into a computer with a microphone and you present the module. You just talk through your slides and you annotate the learning for people. You do the talking and can show and share visuals, which can make a complicated subject seem a lot simpler.

If you're presenting and recording on a screen capture, you'll need relevant software, e.g. ScreenFlow on Mac or Camtasia on Windows. This software will help you present, talk, and move through your slides. I'm not going to teach you how to use the software. There's lots of free online resources available for that. I'm simply giving you the options of how to record your online course on what's available.

Then you need to produce your video in an editor and convert it into a file format that can be uploaded onto your E-Learning platform. This can be done in ScreenFlow or Camtasia.

When building the slides, it's worth investing in some graphic design. Get a graphic designer to create something unique to you. The little illustrations that give people an idea of what it is you're talking about. Obviously, if it's a practical skill you will need to stand in front of a camera, and that camera will need to be recording what you're doing.

Presenting

▶ This is where you talk directly to camera. There is something quite bizarre about recording yourself versus doing a live video. If you are presenting live, the brain has an amazing ability to cope. You survive, you seem to come out with the words in the right place, as if by magic, but when you know you can always do it again there is a tendency not to perform so well. Certainly, recording yourself presenting you will be far more self-critical than if you are voice commentating PowerPoint slides. You will repeat the recording until it is perfect. Unless you are particularly keen to do a presentation style course then I would suggest you start with recording voiceover PowerPoint. Having said that, here are some tips for presenting your recordings:

▶ Think about your appearance.

▶ Find a good background.

▶ Don't worry about the odd mistake, keep going. If you are going to record 120 hours of content, you will need to find momentum and efficient practice of working.

▶ Watch out for your annoying habits:

   » Body twitching

   » Hand clasping

   » Ums and Ahs

   » Repetition of filling words and phrases like "on reflection", "one of the things", "sooo", "aaannnnddd", or "basically"…

You need to think about your presentation style when you're presenting. Make sure that it's clear and you're not muffled with no background noises.

Which is best?

Neither methodology works any better than the other. It's down to personal preference. Sometimes it's nice to have a mix of both. Sometimes you might present in front of a camera, but if there's a more advanced topic and you need to have more detailed notes, then you might want to move to a screen capture, and you can flip between the two and just introduce yourself each time. So, there you go.

Intro & outro

You're going to want an intro and outro. It's a bit of a jingle to tell people that the course is about to start and finish. An intro and outro can be exactly the same music and video piece. We often send our logo off to someone on Fiverr.com and then they turn the logos into a little 3 – 4 second video with some music behind it. Be sure to use copyright free music as it makes a professional start and end to each video. It also signals that your video has started and is finishing rather than just falling off a cliff. It's more comfortable to know that the module has finished.

You'll then need to add this to your video. It's a very simple process. It's quite good to have a logo that represents your business and your brand, and the name of the module of your programme.

Step 5. Tools and outsourcing

Platform

A platform is the system and technology that hosts your content and is intelligent in being able to release content to your members, based on their payments being processed and the length of time you have been enrolled as a customer. For example, Kajabi, Teachable and Click Funnels all have this capability. Having a platform is fundamental to your course, but it's not the platform itself that will make it successful, it's the 3 pillars of success:

1. IP

2. Structure

3. Sales

There are many "off the shelf" platforms that you can use to host your course. You pay a fee to use the software rather than having to invest heavily in building your own, so the start-up costs are really low. I personally use something called Kajabi; you could choose WordPress plugins or ClickFunnels.

The capability of these platforms keeps changing, as they add new releases and develop new smart techniques to stay ahead of their competitors. I use Kajabi because it felt like a platform that was backed by some really friendly, nice people who seemed to care about the small start-up just as much as the million-pound-per-month-revenue customers. They have neat little rewards like rucksacks, water bottles and t-shirts, which make you feel warm and fluffy about the brand. Remember what I said about what the customer needs versus wants. People post their t-shirts, fleeces and rucksacks all over social media, which is great for the Kajabi brand. Do I need a rucksack when I hit $250,000 sales for the first time? No. Do I want one? Hell, yes! Am I proud of what it means? YES.

However, you could also have a whole platform designed for you by a good website and IT company, if you have the budget, though I would really strongly advise against this as it is just not needed. Kajabi has spent millions designing their platform that you can get for a few 100 dollars a month. I see people do this to save monthly running costs, but personally, I think it is a false economy because these e-knowledge platforms have a massive roll-out programme of developments and new improvements.

Whichever platform you choose, I would suggest you record an introduction to your course and load it up to your E-Learning platform and see what it looks like. You'll get a much better idea with practising on that for a couple of hours than having recorded weeks and weeks and weeks of content and then realising that you've got a big, hissing, buzzing noise in the background that's going to distract your customers. Start somewhere.

Outsourcing

I'd like to give you a few ideas of what works for my mentees and what works for me. I believe that business owners and entrepreneurs shouldn't be doing everything. If you do, you are effectively saying you are worth less than minimum wage. There is a lot to do as a working professional nowadays. You can't do everything. I'm not perfect. I can't do everything as well as someone else can. Interestingly, what we are good at normally gives us pleasure and can be enjoyable. If you really hate something or think it's not something you are good at – outsource it.

Make a list of everything you need to do and look at what activities really contribute to your success. Could you afford a few hours a week help to start with? Gradually build up the support as you earn more money.

There are two ways I look at outsourcing:

1. Skills I need

Skills related to online course creation you may want to out-source:

1. **Video editing** – Adding an intro and outro to a video is quite simple on an iPad or computer, but if it is simply too much for you, find someone on Upwork or Fiverr and get them to do it for you.

2. **Graphic design** – Graphic design is worth every penny. If you know nothing about designing, you need a graphic designer on your team. I love that I hand something to our graphic designer, and it comes back looking so professional and amazing.

3. **Platform building** – If you are using one of the mainstream platforms, there are many experts out there that can help you set them up, design them, load content. Most platforms have super users or consultants that you can use to build your course out if you don't have the time or the dedication to learn this stuff.

4. **Downloadable document creation and design** – If you want downloadable spreadsheets, forms, specific calculators or other printable brochures then you could

consider finding an expert who could probably do this ten times faster than you.

5. **Sound stripping from video into audio files** – A lot of people listen to audio tracks, podcasts. It's a really great benefit to have audio files available for your customers to download.

6. **Transcribing for script creation** – If you have recorded a video into an audio file that you think would be useful to have in a text format. You could get a recorded voice memo or file transcribed into text.

7. **Webinar/voiceover recording** – If you are uncomfortable presenting a webinar on your own, you could ask someone else to host you and to prompt and probe at the right points during your webinar. We often have co-hosts on our webinars because it helps to have a conversation instead of a monologue.

Any business skills that could free up your time to enable you to work on your course content:

1. Event scheduling and diary management

2. Bookkeeping

3. Digital marketing – ad creation

4. Graphic design of PowerPoint slides

5. Content Creation for blogs

6. Copywriting for key landing pages and email campaigns

7. Email management – virtual assistant admin

2. Cost of my time

If I can earn more than the hourly rate of the work I am paying for, then I should outsource. I should be earning the highest rate so that I can use that money to pay for the services I need. This could be bookkeeping or admin or something technical. There is an opportunity cost of doing everything yourself (how much you will lose by doing that task when you could have been earning more).

Value your time and energy. Don't do tasks that you could have outsourced and then run out of time and energy to earn money.

SUBSCRIBERS' JOURNEY

Have you ever mapped out the process your typical subscriber goes through? I think it would be interesting to check how many times customers need nudging, prompting or reminding before you get to a sale. Is it enough or too much?

You want to try to make sure that when subscribers come on board, that they get on board successfully. They should get welcome emails as well as emails that congratulate them when they complete a module. Perhaps you might offer a "Welcome to the programme" call.

WHAT ESSENTIALS WILL MAKE YOUR CUSTOMERS' LIVES EASIER?

What do your clients need to get the job done? This might be tools, checklists, scripts, templates, PowerPoints, forms or spreadsheets that you've designed that you could give to them. It might be that they like particular webinars or Q&A sessions that you do. Check back with subscribers.

OTHER RELEVANT CONTENT

Could you bring in more experts that support your subject? One of the things we've done in our property education courses is bring in tax experts or mortgage brokers. You can bring in supporting experts that enrich your programme, but don't necessarily take away from your own content. Perhaps you could choose to pay other subject matter experts to help you?

FINISHING

A month's content or module for your members is the only thing that counts when they are paying you. You can guarantee that if the content disappears, they will stop paying you and ask for refunds. You must fulfil your commitment. I know this is really obvious, but I want to mention it here because far too many people think they can record a few videos and make millions. The reality is it takes planning. You need to outline content, repeat some elements for learning, dig deeper on some parts. You may need to go off on tangents but you will always need to address the essential need of your clients. Don't bother writing half a course. When you start this journey, you need to be prepared for the hard work, you need to be dedicated to finishing the content. Unfortunately, much like a 99% complete book that doesn't have a title and isn't published, it's of no use to anyone unless you finish it.

I suggest you write the content as you go along, when you are starting out, as, not only will a number of paying customers stop you from procrastinating, it also gives you feedback from live customers and members to help you gauge what content is interesting to them.

Writing in this way requires tenacity, discipline and planning. You will need an outline that is detailed enough to know where you are going but also gives you enough space to develop themes as they arise. There is nothing worse than running out of content a few months too early.

EXECUTE
KEY LEARNINGS

1. You should be motivated by your Expressions of Interest, you should not be stuck in perfection, and should be moving into prolific content creation.

2. You need to create the asset. I can't promise that this bit will be easy, just worth it.

3. You will need to find an E-Learning platform that you're comfortable using.

4. You need to create the content; you need to get in front of a camera.

5. You need to break your product down into bite-sized chunks.

6. You'll also want to repeat content, people need the repetition.

7. You'll want to introduce a subject; you'll want to give detail of what they're going to learn and then you summarise it.

8. You launch and deliver.

So, that's it. No excuses; go create.

CHAPTER 14

ENGAGE

"A designer knows he has achieved perfection not when there is nothing left to add, but when there is nothing left to take away."

ANTOINE DE SAINT-EXUPÉRY

WHAT IS ENGAGE?

Engage is ensuring you have a great product and really engaged customers who want to keep paying. It's about serving the customer with the best product you can produce.

The process of engaging involves getting to know your customers and what they value and then empowers you to improve based on their feedback. That feedback is really important for the evolution of your product.

WHY IS IT IMPORTANT TO ENGAGE AND WHAT HAPPENS IF YOU DON'T DO IT?

Engage is about commitment. Engagement is what you get when you create an honest product with integrity and commitment, where it's important to you what outcome your customers and subscribers get from your online course.

Engaging your customers is the only way to get five- to six-figure months. If you have a great product but no engaged customers, you still have no money because your customers will quit your course. Underlying engagement is building a strong asset that delivers great content for your community and gives a great connection to your community.

Good engagement is about making sure you've got a good product, that you've got renewed and refreshed content, that you've got supporting supplementary courses for people that want to keep on working with you and buying from you.

If you get it wrong and don't Engage with your customers, you won't see the increased value from that engagement. If you don't put effort into building and improving your product and community, then you'll find that the lifetime value of your product or customers will be less and you will have to work harder at customer acquisition. People will come on, they won't see the value, and then they'll disappear off. They won't stick around and keep spending. You'll lose the fun factor of your online course. If people leave your course, it's handy to get some feedback and make sure that you understand some of the reasons for subscribers leaving.

CASE STUDY
Solving a problem

When I started working with an expert in diet, we set out a really nice course structure that was all about the nutritionist's expertise and knowledge but not about what the customer wanted. It became difficult to hook customers to join up because we weren't addressing the customers' problems or issues. We fixed this by moving from a message about having better health to addressing stress and low energy issues. We developed a hook that was engaging. The hook is proportionate to the problem. We talked about solving problems in chapter 10. Remember, the bigger the problem, or the more quickly it is worsening, the more motivated a customer is to find a solution. The status quo is the most dangerous. If someone has good health, they have no pain and no signs that they have a problem. We got feedback by the number of subscribers that came on board and we changed the message.

THE 5 STEPS OF ENGAGE

There are various ways to increase engagement in you and your brand and you and your online product.

I will list them out below then cover each point in more detail:

1. Build a community

2. Improve your product

3. Refresh and renew content

4. Add supplementary courses

5. Build a "value chain" of courses and products

Step 1. Build a community

As part of your membership, I encourage you to try to create a community. A community of subscribers will help you deliver your course, but it will also help you create an engaging and valuable place for people to come and share their key learnings and understandings of your programme.

Early on, community became a key component of my product. I bet you can relate to being lonely in business and needing someone to offload problems to. That feeling of being lonely, not sure what mistakes you are making, and wanting to learn tips to accelerate your success.

If you can give people enough value and show them why they should be part of your community, then they will want to belong; they will share with others so that the group exponentially grows in success and progress. It is an eternal circle, based on knowledge, sharing and experience.

Communities provide a place for like-minded people to hang out.

We are all conditioned to look for connection and validation of our thoughts and beliefs. We are drawn to like-minded people. Community is now a huge part of business. If you can grow and Engage a community on social media, this will be the biggest asset you will ever create. It will take some time, but your community will be your customers of the future. They will watch and observe you over time and eventually those that respect your values and build up enough trust will buy from you.

Host your community

There are many ways to host a community, but one of the most successful ways is probably through a Facebook group. There are software platforms that specifically host a forum and community type arrangement, but one of the things you have to consider is how often people would come out of their normal day to day platforms and go into another platform just to Engage in this community. Very often, things like a community platform sat on a website or app will be forgotten. Therefore, we use Facebook groups.

Our Facebook groups are typically locked down so that only members who are subscribing and paying can be invited in and contribute. We load content directly into that community group as videos and other posts that help our subscribers move forward. Post content in your Facebook group but keep pushing your subscribers back to the E-Learning platform for already recorded content. Keep pushing them back to your content, where your classes and your online courses are held.

Use your community

Use your community to build and develop:

a. **Case studies** of successful students. People love case studies. Success case studies give other members inspiration and ideas, help attract potential subscribers who can relate to someone else's problem ("Well maybe this could work for me because it worked for them.") and help you attract partnerships as well because they will give your product credibility.

b. **Feedback** on course content. Feedback shared on the course into a community gives others an opportunity to comment on what has worked for them and also helps identify strategies that are working and new tips.

c. **Open and honest communication** with members. Trust is built on honest communications. Trust is built over a period of time with good communication, tone and body language. That's why video is so powerful; your customer still experiences your tone and body language. Their trust level builds to a high level and then the customer buys.

Help your community

There are lots of different things that you can do to help your community move forward. In any community, try and delight your subscribers, make sure that you have some bonuses they weren't expecting. You want to over deliver. Give lots and lots of content directly into the community. If you feel you're charging enough, then perhaps you might want to think about what you can do outside of a platform such as regular or monthly calls, or Zooms, or group coaching calls, where people get to interact and come and ask questions. And remember, if one person asks you questions then everybody benefits.

Size counts, so keep growing your community

To begin with, you might find that you don't have enough customers to create an interesting community (it will be too quiet), so you might want to wait until launch day to actually create your community. Once you have a reasonable group, it can be used as an advertising tool. Potential customers see how big and active it is and want to come and hang out there. If you see that a community group has got 100 members in it, for instance, you will know that this is a course programme that 100 other people have subscribed to, and that in itself will give people security and reassurance that actually this is a programme of worth and value.

Step 2. Improve your product

If you avoided perfectionism in the name of getting your product launched, then this might be the time to go back and check all your content and modules are consistent, the quality is all the same, the content is up to date, etc.

a. **Improve content where any confusion exists**
You will probably have had some comments and feedback and clarity around what works well for some modules and you will know what needs improving. It's worth keeping on top of these changes. It's also worth going back through your content and refreshing what you have already written. Record new content, add bonuses. If you help one person, perhaps on a 1-2-1 call, then see if there is any improvement to the content.

b. **Build new products around the needs of members**
You might realise that you do something that is so natural to you that others don't understand or relate to it. This discovery could significantly improve your product and add

new revenue streams and increase the customer lifetime value, e.g. if you use LinkedIn well when recruiting staff, perhaps you could teach LinkedIn skills.

c.   **Ensure all content meets consistent format and structure**

Quality can be a procrastinator's crutch. They never produce anything until it is perfect. The very act of producing something means you have produced something that doesn't meet your vision. If you did take an inconsistent approach to content creating, then go back and put some consistent quality standards in place. Sometimes, for whatever reason, the video or the audio setting got changed and the quality is not as good as it should be. You may have accepted this in the short term but go back and refresh.

d.   **Tangibles. Making the product tangible**

In a digital world, it helps give your product tangibility if you can create downloadable workbooks or spreadsheets that can be printed. Create downloads/workbooks/audio to download. If you can surround people with multi-device experiences, you create extra value.

Step 3. Refresh and renew content – the life of your asset

Your product will evolve over time, it's just like in nature. Competition and other environmental pressures can cause a species to become threatened. Products need to evolve. They need to adapt. Digital assets have fantastic paybacks. The cash that you put out to create the digital assets in online courses can be quickly returned to you in a few months or years. You may have spent a few hundred pounds to get that back in a few months. Whereas a property or physical asset can have a much longer return on cash flow and payback.

It's not going to be unusual to need to evolve your product every few years. Competitors – who may have more time to record better content than you, write more blogs, attract more customers, etc – join the market. You just need to consider what will be the next version of your product. What is the trend at the moment? Where will my business be in 7-10 years' time?

What needs refreshing in your course? What content might you need to go back to and re-record? What parts of the course have caused confusion with your subscribers? What do they love? Has any terminology changed? What would you do differently if you were starting again? What extra modules should you create?

1. **Give value to new and updated techniques and tips**

2. **Provide new content**

Keep your content refreshed and keep it up to date. And remember, be prolific, don't be a perfectionist. Make sure you keep editing and adding new content. Put it in your platform, and also keep reminding your database or membership that the content is there.

Step 4. New supplementary courses

Create and produce new courses that supplement your existing one. There are two areas for you to explore.

1. **Existing areas**

   You can branch off a bit or go a bit deeper in one area, both of which can either become new standalone courses on their own or sit alongside your product and you can add them as bonus modules to delight your customers.

   a. **Broader support of your subject**

      You might get some feedback from your engagement process that highlight subscribers' lack of understanding in one area, so you might want to branch off into a side subject with lots of different avenues you could go down. For example, in a course about how to create a fashion business, you find Instagram ads are particularly difficult for customers so you might explore a basics course of Instagram ads for fashion businesses as a small mini course.

   b. **Deeper learning**

      You might get feedback that you need to go deeper on a certain topic. We can use the same analogy with Instagram ads. If you've got an Instagram ad course, you might have a basics course and then go into specific, detailed ways of targeting and retargeting in ads and perhaps sub niches of fashion industries. How different demographics use Instagram or not, etc.

2. **New relevant subject areas**

   This is about growing in new directions. Say you have a course on Facebook ads that is going well so you might want to create a course on LinkedIn ads or Twitter ads or Google ads or any other media where the pay per click common theme is there. You might want to do something completely different, of course, but with the same overarching objectives.

Step 5. Build a "value chain" of courses and products

In every successful business, there is a chain of products from the cheapest to the most expensive. As customers gain trust through purchasing items along the chain, the lifetime value of the customer increases. If you buy a candle from a fashion designer and then you go and buy a scarf, then you might buy a top and then you buy the full outfit and designer handbag. You trust not only the retailer but your own buying choices. Maybe you only spent £20 on the candle, but by the end you were happy spending £2000 on the handbag. At each stage your relationship with the brand increases and your willingness to spend more increases with every transaction.

How does a value chain work?

The idea around building a value chain of products is that you have products that are all formed on the same content and information that continue to give your clients and customers value in different packages and formats. A value chain of products is essential for your business growth; it could get you to seven-figure years.

Every part of the business increases because the chances of survival of the business all depends on the connection of the products within the chain. Because you are only as strong as the weakest link, the chain relies on all the strength of the links before it, and any new links added to the end should extend your customers' lifetime value. It is the individual parts that make up the overall strength of the chain.

The value chain of an online course

1. Your hook

2. Small DIY product

3. Ongoing learning

4. Done together product

5. Mastermind

6. 1-2-1 coaching

If you develop a family of products, you will open up the value creation process in your business. You just need to expand your value in different ways:

▶ Add more of yours or another trainer's time

▶ Add more content

▶ Positioning, online or face to face live content.

DIAGRAM: BUILD A VALUE CHAIN

1-2-1 coaching
- Most expensive • Your time • Bespoke advice

Mastermind
- 1-2-Many Training • Members dictate a lot of content
- Application only, high price point • Additional support when required
- Ongoing

Done together product
- 1-2 Many Training • Fixed Course length • Contact and
- Structured • Deep dives on content   connection with you

Ongoing learning
- Content Ongoing • Monthly low level subscription
- Community forum • Additional support, timetabled by you

Small DIY product
- Small sale £ • Small Mini Course
- Asset that delivers without you • Discreet Quick Learning

Your hook
- Lead Magnet • Free Content • Podcast • Book • Blogs

In accountancy, we call this value-based accounting – the value and pricing increases and moves from one product to another. I worked in a construction business and we had stone that was produced from a quarry and was sold as bulk volume. It was washed, crushed and sold in different sizes. The stone was added to cement and concrete was made. Additives were added, and then special mortar products were developed. Bitumen was added to make tarmac. Labour was added to create a road tarmac contract team. Value was created from a common product.

1. Your hook

Is a small product that provides a customer with almost instant gratification, typically for free or a small spend. It is very easy to consume. This small product gets the customer on the hook. Sometimes on social media this is called clickbait. It is the hook to get people to stop and spend some time consuming your content.

2. Small DIY product

You might have a spreadsheet tool or a mini course for people to purchase or download for free on your website to get them interested in your core product, and to make sure you can add their email addresses to the mailing list to let them know about your other products, promotions, etc...

3. Ongoing learning

In my experience, there are a good 80% of people that will never buy your core high priced product from you. They can't justify it. It's not high enough on their values and priorities for them to consider the solution value for money. They don't buy at this level. These people may never purchase any consultancy from me, but they buy my online course (which requires a modest financial commitment). This is perfect for them because it's affordable and still solves their problem. For those who may go on to purchase higher-ticket items, this is an easy and gentle start to our relationship of working together. It is also ideal for those unable to attend live training.

4. Done together product

The next level of support is done together, where you might offer some time live as a coach or mentor to enhance their experience of the DIY course. There are different ways of supplementing your product by adding time with you. Blending the two approaches bridges the gap between where customers want and need support. This could be you supporting your members with group coaching calls, a regular video call or you might offer them email support. Products that require you to deliver content live (e.g. a call) require more of your time, and you can charge a little more. You want to leverage your time as often as possible; that's either a one to many call or live class or online content.

5. Mastermind

My live classroom-based programme is essentially for customers who have been through our done together products. A mastermind is getting your customers together and helping the group. The principle behind it is that when we come together, we are greater than the sum of our individual parts. The mastermind group contains super positive, well connected, knowledgeable and motivated people. I love mastermind groups and hosting them for our mentees.

6. 1-2-1 coaching

At the final level is a 1-2-1 product. For most people this is you taking their problem and actively solving it with your knowledge and products to give them more certainty around the outcome they want. 1-2-1 is obviously the full solution, and each level has a different price tag attached to it. So, think about how you might put this into your business and how you might develop this. Don't undersell your time.

This should be your most expensive product because it will involve a lot of your time and systems and their issues become yours to solve. For example, this would be me actively taking your content and putting it into an online course and running your membership for you. As you can imagine, I would want a lot more money to achieve that for you compared to teaching you to do it yourself. However, I am prepared to offer this for the right price as I do like working with people directly and enjoy the satisfaction of helping people. Because I love working with people, and I love business, this gives me a way of spending some of my time doing what I enjoy.

⚷

ENGAGE
Key Learnings

Now you have perfected your product(s) you are ready to tell the world about it and Extend. There are lots of different things that you can do to help your community move forward. In any community, try to delight your subscribers. You want to make sure that you have some bonuses they weren't expecting. You want to over deliver. And if you feel you're charging enough, then perhaps you might want to think about what you can do outside of a platform such as regular or monthly calls, or group coaching calls, where people get to interact and come and ask questions. Create great products and invest in a community, it will serve you well.

1. How quickly can you start earning a six-figure sum from online courses?

2. Engage is all about getting your act together and getting your product right and continuing to improve.

3. What small changes can you make that can have a huge impact on your income?

4. Can you outsource and bring in third-party suppliers? How will this help you improve the return on investment and maximise your income fast.

CHAPTER 15

EXTEND

"Keep your sales pipeline full by prospecting continuously. Always have more people to see than you have time to see them."

BRIAN TRACY

WHAT IS EXTEND?

The process of extending is to answer the following questions:

▶ How do I move from the launch stage of my product and now start moving into five-figure months or more?

▶ How do I evolve?

▶ What help do I need to continue to scale?

Our first goal is to get you up to £1k per calendar month in regular subscriptions, then we take you up the level and we start to Extend you to £2k to £5k then £5k to £10k and through that you're going to Extend your range and reach more people.

The ultimate aim is to try to get you to over £10k per month.

A lot of this is about testing and measuring what works and what key things you can do to make the boat go faster.

Success typically isn't linear, it's not straight lined, it comes in steps. Big steps that you need to really climb up on to see what's coming next.

How are you going to climb that next step?

What do you need in your business?

What support do you need to get to the six-figure months, not the five-figure months?

WHY IS EXTEND IMPORTANT AND WHAT HAPPENS IF YOU DON'T DO IT?

Extending your product gives you the capability to invest in your course and to do exciting things to grow and scale it, which is both exciting for the course and your life, for more money, more fun. Extending your product helps you keep your course alive and vibrant. With more money coming into the course, you can take a higher income and still have money to invest in researching partnership opportunities, new pipeline development, ad agency costs, new equipment and copywriting.

If you don't Extend your product into the world you can have the best product but a lot of people who need it will never find out about it. If you don't Extend, the product will lose energy and die off in the next 3-5 years. It needs a certain amount of investment, nurturing and growth to get some momentum.

This is the exciting part about growing – you can leverage the asset to the fullest because to scale and grow now doesn't require massive delivery effort from you. It does require you to track and identify your numbers and test and measure.

THE 5 STEPS OF EXTEND

There are five tactics we employ to Extend the income generation from your programme. Extension is about reaching as far as you can with your product.

1. Increase the value of your funnel

2. Increase the number of people in your funnel

3. Use someone else's funnel

4. Charge more

5. Sell more

   a. Sell to those on your list who have not already bought

   b. Upsell more to customers who have bought or engaged in your product

Step 1. Increase the value of your funnel

Could we improve everything in your course funnel by 10%?

Don't underestimate the difference between a 20% conversion and a 30% conversion, because whilst it may only be a 10% increase, it is a 50% improvement in the amount of people coming into your membership. If you could improve the amount of people registering their email address with you every day by 50%, and instead of having 20, you'd have 30, that would create your exponential growth. Take this stuff seriously, track your numbers, and really get into this with a return on investment mindset.

DIAGRAM: INCREASE YOUR FUNNEL

SALES PROCESS	SALES RESULTS
Clicks on ad	5,000
2%	
Gives email for a report	100
20%	
Reads email and joins webinar	20
30%	
Buys course from webinar	6

10% INCREASE IN CONVERSION RATES

SALES PROCESS	SALES RESULTS
Clicks on ad	5,500
2.2%	
Gives email for a report	121
22%	
Reads email and joins webinar	27 (Rounded up)
33%	
Buys course from webinar	9

50% INCREASE IN SALES

This diagram shows the number of sales that would result from a 10% increase in conversion rate. If this was three extra sales per month, that would be an extra 36 customers in 12 months x £100 (if your course was priced at £100 per month). That would equate to £3600. Of course, some would unsubscribe and some would stay and there is layering and compound effect of the growth, but you can see how powerful even a modest increase in conversion rate can be.

This diagram explores the opportunity of improving each conversion rate by 10%. The overall result is you have 50% more sales as a result of marginal improvements throughout the funnel. The more steps in the funnel and the more you can improve the conversion rates, the greater the impact.

On average, we sign up 20-30% of webinar attendees on a low-ticket item, such as a discounted trial for 28 days. If we get those 20-30% of people to convert, we then know from our statistics about 14% fall out of the trial (churn). This means that 14% subscribe and never go past trial of 28 days. Over time, even after 12 months, we retain typically 13% – 28% of all subscribers, which is pretty amazing.

Then, we would calculate the lifetime value. Don't forget, at the beginning of your course, your lifetime value should go up until you are well into the first 12 months. You're looking for that continual growth because, remember, as you're writing each month, people that subscribed maybe one, two, three months ago are getting content that you have only just written.

If you sell bigger and larger products to people, then the Lifetime Value (LTV) just goes up and continues. Use the statistics to scale and move through the business and keep growing because you can test and measure different strategies.

We test and measure our different audiences and different opening offers. We might add new modules or new bonuses to the course to see how well the evolution of our product keeps going. We might sell the whole 12 months' content. We might offer a discount for people who have, perhaps, exited the course because the timing wasn't right for them, and we might then phone them up a couple of months later and offer them the whole programme but with lifetime access.

Improve your copy to increase your conversion rate

The way you communicate with people about what you do: the words, images and media you use, make a massive difference to whether people sign up and stay signed up. So, it's important to learn more about how to write good copy that sells to improve your website, landing pages and copywriting.

If possible, you can pay a professional to take a look at your landing page and improve the copy you originally wrote. They may also be able to help with other messaging such as adverts, social media posts, etc.

Although you did your best with the original landing page, now you have some cash, pay a professional to make it convert better.

Use follow-up sequences to increase conversion rate

They say in sales, "the fortune is in the follow-up". An automated follow-up sequence is a system that automatically sends out emails from pre-written templates based on triggers from your customer or set to go out at a certain time. If you have a new subscriber, you can send out weekly emails of encouragement and these are all sent automatically. You can send reminders if people put stuff into their basket and don't complete the sale; this is an automated follow-up sequence, also known as an abandoned cart follow-up.

For example, if somebody purchases a book from you, then you send them six or seven pre-written emails that come out in a timely fashion after the first initial contact. The person buying the small item can be automatically put into another sales process to sell a bigger ticket item. Depending on which source of research you quote, they say it takes over 5 – 7 touches to make a sale. People need to build trust to buy from you, especially for larger purchases.

Sales are really about following up. People are busy. So, you do need to make sure that you're in their inbox, regularly telling them about your content and showing them your offers and products. You need to make sure you're not leaving money on the table by ensuring you consistently do the follow-up properly so that you can convert to a sale.

Research by Insidesales.com found if you follow-up a web lead within five minutes, you're nine times more likely to convert it. That's stunning.

Follow-up sequences are readily available on most of the platforms. On the one I use, we have conditional targeted follow-up actions (meaning we send them different emails depending on how they have behaved). We send out follow-up sequences when people subscribe, when new content is released on the course they have purchased, or when they have been inactive for a few weeks. This allows us to keep customers engaged. For example, we might follow-up with people who bought a book, by sharing how they can download the audiobook. Then we might send them another email asking how they are finding the book, etc. Then we share our other products.

You could have a scenario where, depending on the action in the email opened, the next email the user gets is different. If, for instance, I send my list an email about how to overcome the tech aspects of presenting your online course, and they open it, then I know they are interested and can then send them a follow-up email on tech options. Whereas, if I'd have just sent them another email about how to get their content online, it's less relevant. They're less likely to open and less likely to think I'm with them in terms of being able to solve their problem.

Step 2. Increase the number of people in your funnel

Increasing the number of people in your funnel is another way of growing your course. However, because of the funnelling affect, you do need to pour a lot more in the top.

A 50% increase in the top has the same effect as an increase in conversion of 10%.

Please see the example below, which brings in an extra six customers a month. This is the same result as increasing the conversion rate as shown on page 322. 50% increase in the top is much harder to achieve, is more expensive and can be sensitive to short term variations.

That's why we suggest you put aside at least 10% of your revenue to advertise on social media platforms, to run events and to drag more people in the top.

Extend your mailing list

In my experience, emails are the best conversion method to get your prospects to take action. It is one of the most successful ways, and I mean head and shoulders above every other method of getting a conversion. Most sales start through an email address.

A great idea is to get people's email addresses and then you own the data. This means you can market back to your list as often as you want, all for the cost of running a CRM/emailing system. You have to be compliant with data protection law and

DIAGRAM: BUILD A VALUE CHAIN

SALES PROCESS	SALES RESULTS
Landing page	5,000
2%	
Gives email for a report	100
20%	
Reads email and joins webinar	20
30%	
Buys course from webinar	6

50% INCREASE IN TRAFFIC AT THE TOP

SALES PROCESS	SALES RESULTS
Landing page	7,500
2%	
Gives email for a report	150
20%	
Reads email and joins webinar	30
30%	
Buys course from webinar	9

50% INCREASE IN SALES

GDPR law in Europe, but we still find that this is the highest performing route to market. If you need to do double opt-ins or get permission to add people to your marketing list, do that. Email marketing is not dead. There are more barriers to getting your list but consider that less people will be doing this and those that do subscribe are probably super motivated to work with you.

Why do emails work? If you think about what's happening in your customers' minds, an email that's sent to you in your inbox, it's like a letter. It's like a pile of paper that needs to be dealt with on your desk. Physically, it's not there, but actually people do go through their inboxes and clear them down to zero. Particularly, when they're in a work mode.

Email is one of those things where you have the undivided attention of your prospect for a few seconds. You're not in a Facebook forum, you're not on LinkedIn, you're not on Twitter, and if you've ever seen the speed at which Twitter moves through tweets, you'll realise that you have a very fleeting few seconds of attention with somebody and there are many, many other ways of being distracted. Primarily, when people are on social media forums, and that includes LinkedIn, they're there to serve themselves. They're there to get entertainment, to perhaps browse job offers or to snoop on other people. Email is different because people are trying to deal with and action the email as it comes into their inbox. They're having to assess whether it's an opportunity or not, whether they are interested in it or not. They have to make that decision.

It's not uncommon to achieve 40 to 50% click-through rates from existing members for each email you send. Up selling to existing members through emails is normally very successful. For non-members, open rates tend to be lower but still good at 20 to 30% of email content, and that is sometimes higher depending on how fresh the audience is and how much content they've had from you.

Email is the best communication tool for getting people to your events. Social media is good for building awareness of you and your brand. You can use social media to get people to raise their hands and say they are interested. Email is 40 times more effective at acquiring new customers than Facebook or Twitter[18].

Utilise your mailing list

Once you have email addresses you need to use them. Don't sit on a huge email list and never email people. The optimum frequency for emailing is the one you can be the most consistent in delivering. If you can consistently send an email every day to your list, send an email every day. If you can do this once a week or every other day, do that. Once you have some understanding of the behaviours of your audience, measure what works and then scale. The problem is you never know when your prospect is ready to buy. You have to keep doing the best you can and test and measure your email campaigns. It's better to do something and work on the consistency model than to worry if your email has the right title and is sent out at 5.02 am with video links. You can get perfect but get out there first. Email marketing works. I've tracked the size of our email list for some time. It is a key focus of our business.

Getting your subscribers ATTENTION

▶ **Timing**. Most emails are read between 5:00 – 6:00 AM.

▶ **Wording**. Some words work better than others. For instance, "connect" or "apply" work better than "join" or "confirm" in terms of your keywords in subject lines.

▶ **Capitalization**. Amazingly, using capitals in an email title is supposed to hurt the response rate by 30%, according to some analysis done by boomerang[19].

▶ **Video**. 7 in 10 B2B buyers watch a video of some sort during their buying process, according to HubSpot.

▶ **Personalising**. Make emails personal. According to Experian, emails with personalised subject lines are 7% more likely to be opened[20].

If you are emailing using CRM or mailing software (e.g. Mailchimp), you should be able to insert name fields into the email titles, body and text.

Emailing a section of your list based on the actions they have taken is super effective. Also called Segmented campaigns, this can drive a 760% increase in revenue[21].

You need to be doing all you can to get as many email addresses as possible. A lot of the other things we're about to cover are ultimately working towards that single goal of getting more email addresses, to then use.

Develop more lead magnets to get more email addresses

A lead magnet is something of value that you put on a landing page to give in exchange for a prospect's email address. A lead magnet can be anything. There just needs to be a trip line for your prospect to arrive and then exchange their details for your FREE offer. Some examples include:

▶ an eBook

▶ a comprehensive guide

▶ a document of tips

▶ an infographic of your process or methodology

▶ a link to a podcast episode

▶ a report or a white paper which includes facts and statistics so that your customer feels that they are on top of all the knowledge that they need

▶ a seat at your next webinar

▶ pre-recorded lessons or video

▶ slides or a mini presentation

For example, I tell my prospects I've got a particular report on the top 10 tips for monetising your knowledge and putting it online. This appeals to a prospect who just wants to find out a bit more about me to see if they like what I am saying and value my information, so they give me their email address and download my report.

They're on the hook for this and they know that they might be getting some more follow-up information from me too, but they're happy to go with it because I'm not going to spam them, I'm not going to sell their email address on to anyone else, I am just providing value. I'm going to follow the GDPR guidelines and have a privacy policy that they can click-through to, which then gives them reassurance that they can exchange their email address. And of course, they can always unsubscribe at any point.

Know your cost of customer acquisition before spending anything on adverts

You can get more people into your funnel by spending more on things like Facebook ads, Google ads, and SEO. Before you increase any spending on this, you need to know your cost of acquisition (how much you have to spend to get one paid up customer) and your customer lifetime value.

This is a real funnel that we have used in the past. On the diagram below, you can see from the FB ad costs, our LTV calculated by the system and I have included the landing page conversion image. This is real but I am also aware that it is a lot of money. Our product price is typically between £49 – £250 per month depending on what offer we get a subscriber in on.

If you know you can get 100 people to your landing page from social media and then 10 leave an email address, you have a 10% conversion rate (in the example above this was 11%). If you email 100 people on your email list and 40 people join your webinar, you then have to work out how many people might convert on the webinar into a paid subscriber. And if that's eight people (20%), then your ultimate funnel needs 100 clicks on your landing page to get the people that started at the top and get eight people out of the bottom. You would then need to think about how much that costs you. In the example above it was costing £1.50 per lead from Facebook.

Cost of acquisition of your customer

In this example it cost £1.50 per lead on Facebook adverts. This is a very cheap lead cost because it is targeted at existing website visitors and a customer lookalike audience. I have noticed FB leads increasing in cost as more and more advertisers use the platform and compete, but I wanted to show you a real example. If 100 opt into an email list, that will cost you £150. From the 100 people who subscribe to your email list, only five join a webinar and only one buys. So that means it cost you £150 to get one purchase. This is your cost of acquisition of your customer. The really clever thing is now you have another 99 emails of the 100 you got from Facebook that haven't bought from you yet as well, and over time you can follow-up and they may buy from you in the future.

You won't know how your LTV is settling out for a while. It will keep changing, as the life of your customers does. Even

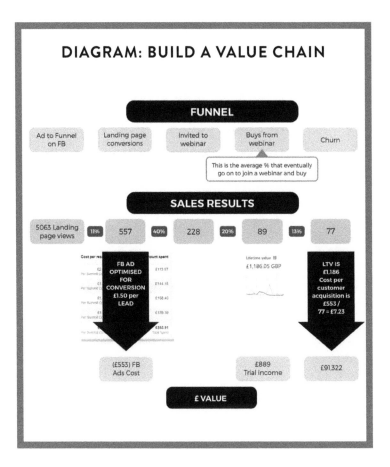

though I have been doing this for many years, we still have customers who have joined from the very first month.

This knowledge and information enables you to develop a funnel and a system that you can ramp up because you can-prove all the way through that you're getting the conversions and you can test and measure and improve them.

SOME IDEAS TO TEST
AND MEASURE

- You might want to split 50% of your FB budgets and trial different initial payment amounts or free trials

- Test different images

- Test different copy/text

- Test different audiences

- You could try different landing pages and test which converts better

- Try different lead magnets

Little tweaks like this will enable you to ramp up and put more spend at the top of your funnel so that you can then effectively get more out of the bottom. You create a cash machine in your business. These key metrics will give you lots of ideas and lots of signposts of where to spend the money.

Facebook ads

Facebook adverts can be used to drive more people into your funnel, whether that's an advert for your course or another of your lead magnets. Facebook ads target people based on their interests and past behaviours, meaning you can find someone who wasn't looking for your product but would be an ideal customer. Facebook ads can be very complex. Facebook is also the biggest of data giants, making it the best at putting your adverts in front of your best prospects. It is a very powerful tool.

You can spend a lot of money on Facebook without even thinking about it. You can put £100 on there and Facebook will do a great job of spending your money as fast as you allow it to. The thing with Facebook is they are running ads to their audience and they're doing that to enable them to provide a free platform of entertainment. They have two key audiences to satisfy:

▶ **People seeking entertainment.** Their job is to keep their viewers on Facebook for as long as possible, entertaining them and giving them content for as much time as the user is prepared to give the Facebook platform.

▶ **People seeking sales (advertisers).** Facebook is not free. They monetise the platform by selling advertising space to businesses.

Facebook has to serve both audiences and in doing so it likes certain things because the audience that consumes information likes certain things, e.g. video. Video on Facebook costs very little to promote and you can typically get views of your video for a penny or a cent a view, and this is a very cheap way of advertising. Facebook makes this way of advertising very cheap because consumers like video. When video comes up in the feed, the attention of that person is to automatically stop to see what's going to happen next. Video becomes a very easy format for Facebook to give to their consumers from their advertisers.

However, Facebook doesn't like their audience being taken off Facebook and onto your own website. It's going to cost you more if you're using Facebook as part of a funnel to get people to engage with your website (either to make a purchase or download a lead magnet).

One of the best ways to get traction around your product is to put videos in front of people and track who's watched those videos, because video views are cheap on Facebook. Facebook will keep that information. They won't tell you exactly who's watched it, even though they do know, but they will allow you to put another video in front of that person. This is done through something called custom audiences; you go into the engagement video builder and you look at who's engaged with your video at so many different points, then you build your unique audience.

Ramp up your return on investment

We went through an example before where potentially you put £553 into advertising and had a customer acquisition cost of £7.23. Due to the lifetime value of your customer, you might get £1186 at the other end. This is the cash machine and you want to know what buttons to press to get the cash out of the machine. Don't think this is going to go away and it's too complicated, because more and more small businesses are going to embrace the Facebook advertising platform and be able to use it. There is a unique opportunity at the moment to embrace Facebook ads because they will get more expensive as more businesses pile into them.

You're going to be able to get super clear on your audience and your niche and who converts the best. But you've got to do the work and the analysis and track back who's doing what. Embrace the data and Facebook.

SEO

Another major traffic source is SEO – that's Search Engine Optimisation. If you have a how-to product or can think of how-to questions that support your course, then SEO might be ideal. Typically, people turn to Google to work out "how" to do something. If you have your website and your keywords all lined up to tell Google what you do, then you can attract traffic to your website and get people to engage with you. I outsource my SEO to professionals. SEO comes into its own when you have a mature product and website that you can regularly add to with blogs and drive traffic to the website. The search engines have algorithms that change regularly, and that's why experts are great to help you rank in search results.

Google adverts

Google ads can drive traffic to your site based on the key-words someone types in. If they are not searching, then you cannot advertise to them. It's a great research tool actually because if people aren't searching for what you offer, you're unlikely to get those five-figure months. You could do some initial testing just to see how many searches are coming up, and that would give you some great ideas of what keywords are out there and what questions are being asked.

If you type the start of a question or key subject into the Google search bar, then Google provides you with a few frequent search suggestions. Google is also quite good at helping you understand what people are searching for.

https://trends.google.com/trends. This gives you lots of information. It can help you write content based on the questions you know people are asking. You can use this information to write blogs and articles that raise your profile as the expert.

Google ads normally have an introductory offer. You can typically get £100 to start some ads. It's simple enough to get started and generate some click-throughs and website views but I think if you are going to spend a lot of money then you should contact a professional or outsource through Fiverr.com or Upwork.com.

Step 3. Use someone else's funnel

A game changer in getting to five-figure months is using things like JVs, affiliates or essentially other people's lists. One of the key limiting factors in your business might be the size of your list and how quickly you can grow it. You might do this really informally, for example, someone recommends you to their customers verbally or on their newsletters, blogs, etc. However, this could be more formal with a joint venture structure or affiliates. I will explain in more detail how both work:

Joint ventures

A joint venture is a business relationship created by two or more parties, generally on a profit share or revenue share basis. Each party brings something to the relationship. There are three things that are needed in considering a joint venture: the product, the distribution channel and the brand.

1. Your course is the product

2. Distribution channels can be;

    - Databases

    - Email lists

    - Own subscribers

    - Followers

    - Listeners

    - Viewers

3. Brand can be; (this might be you already, but you may look to others who aren't monetising their brand)

    - Influencers or celebrities on social media

    - Business recognised leaders who have qualifications and certifications

    - Experts

- Book authors
- Speakers

If your email list isn't growing as fast as you'd like, I would suggest you hunt out everybody that has a list.

PROCESS TO ENGAGE
A JV PARTNER

1. Design a brochure and outline the benefits to your potential JV partners of what the benefits and opportunities of working with you might be.

2. Do some research online or get someone on Upwork to go and find all the influencers or JV partners you want to potentially work with. Get their email addresses and contact if possible.

3. Send them your brochure about working together and ask for an opportunity to call them and discuss further.

4. When you have that discussion, ask your partner to:

   a. Send an email to their list that would involve you then selling these people on to a webinar.

    b. Review your webinar slides and course, so that these partners know their customers are going to get value from your course.

    c. Agree a fee split – can be 50/50 or it can be 25/75. It depends on you. I always find 50/50 is so much easier to negotiate, it seems fair. If you have a number of opportunities to JV then you can push back on the JV share.

4. If your JV partner is willing to trial this, I would make it as easy as possible for them to send people to you. Write the emails, the follow-ups and the brochures or branding documents.

5. Put together some sort of agreement; it will make your JV partner feel more comfortable about fulfilling their obligations. You can put it on an electronic signing website like DocuSign to make it feel official.

It's not about working with as many affiliates as you can, it's about finding a good fit.

Affiliate marketing

An affiliate scheme is the process of obtaining a customer from another person or company promoting your products. You find an affiliate who has your ideal customer database but is not competing with you, and you ask them to promote it to others and they will earn a piece of your profit for each sale that you make. If, for example, you are selling a gardening flowerbed design course, you might approach a vegetable gardening magazine. There might be a conflict if you provide a magazine that gives lots of free content about vegetable gardens but potentially there isn't and since a vegetable garden magazine subscriber might be interested in designing a flowerbed then you could both win out of that relationship. We work with many partners who we earn thousands of pounds from selling our products to their lists and we share this income with them, but we are still thousands of pounds better off.

Process to set up an affiliate relationship

You would find affiliates in the same way as you might find JV partners. Working with affiliates has to be based on a huge amount of trust and you need to find a partner who potentially has a non-conflicting business or other interest that works for them.

1. Find affiliates with your ideal audience where your products don't compete.

2. Agree a percentage of the income.

3. Remember to explain the benefit of online courses and online memberships – that you are offering somebody else a recurring income and sustainable income source.

4. Always think about how you can achieve more together. Whilst there might be some reluctance from others to

market your course on their list, you've really got to work on how you present your offer to other people's customers.

5. Build up a relationship whereby you become a trusted partnership and people see your value.

Think about who could be affiliates. Stop now and write down five or six names that come into your head. Remember, these must be people that have the right audience for you. If you're running a Woman in Business leadership campaign, you might work with somebody who is a personal fashion shopper or a shopper for a busy high-exec lady. There would be two different ways that you'd have complementing products, but you'd essentially have the same audience.

Don't be afraid to give away quite a substantial amount of your income to your partner. One of the benefits of your partnership offer is that your partner will be receiving recurring income as well. That might be a huge benefit to them, knowing they've got X-thousands of pounds coming to them every month, regardless of what they do each month.

You might actually become a significant revenue for your partner or affiliates. Open your mind up to how much you might give away but also to the fact that you're holding a significant amount of knowledge.

You could also let your affiliate partner join your course free of charge, so they get a feel for what's involved and the quality of your product. All those things work really well.

Step 4. Charge more

Scaling up and getting more and more people in your funnel is one option, or have you thought about just increasing your prices? Could you charge more? You will have had an early bird price and maybe also experimented with special discounts and deals, but now it's time to think about offering a higher price rather than a lower one. It may sound strange, but if I told you there were two courses you could do with me online and these were the prices:

1. £80 per month

2. £200 per month

What would you think about the quality of these two courses? I've told you nothing else other than the price. Most people make the assumption that the higher price course is better. Both courses could be exactly the same. Price isn't as important as you think it is for people to buy. Price is important to you. You want to be able to deliver at a price that can afford you. The perception of the value your customer gets is important.

Just think about that for a minute...

Think about your pricing offer.

Most people respond with the idea that actually the £200 product has more content and more value.

Sometimes pricing products too cheaply infers that there is something of less value in your product. Don't be too scared to push your prices up and actually offer value but earn more income.

You don't need to read many reviews to realise that price and satisfaction are completely unrelated. It's unlikely that you will see: "10 out of 10. The product wasn't brilliant, it wasn't really what I needed, but it was cheap, so I gave it 10 out of 10!"

We all have opinions about things, even when they are free (Facebook videos and posts, YouTube videos, TED talks) and we never give anything the thumbs up emoji just because it was free.

The opposite review would be: "I'm only rating this product 5 out of 10 stars because it was really expensive, even though it solved the most impossible challenge for me." It's just as unlikely.

Once your customers have had some value from you, that could be content or a free white paper, keep selling to these customers and start exchanging products for money.

Once you have had some students get results, it's easier to prove the value of your teaching and you can then start charging more.

This is especially true of your customers, who can earn more after completing your course, and you can prove that previous customers have done so. Obviously, it's not your responsibility for them to complete the course, but it is your responsibility to give them the right content to achieve that. If you feel you provide that, then your price can almost be as high as your value given.

Even if your course isn't focused on helping people earn more, having testimonials or case studies from people who have completed the course and seen positive results (whether that is in their guitar playing, water colour painting, meditating, weight, emotional improvement, confidence, etc) will help prove your value, and it can all be leveraged to increase your price.

Step 5. Sell more

This is one of the pillars of the process as per chapter 10. I wanted to mention it again now because I am keen that you sell as much as you can. Whatever your goal, either hitting five-figure months or even six-figure months, at each stage the sales process will need to ramp up. Find ways to get out and sell more. A lot of business owners will try to do anything but sell. They have an aversion to it.

SELL MORE BY DOING MORE SALES PITCHES AND PRESENTATIONS

- Do regular webinars

- Host livestreams on FB

- Post videos on LinkedIn

- Do live events on YouTube

- Give a presentation at a local interest group or small business forum

- Hold regular 2-hour seminars or any other presentations

- The more you do, the more you will sell

TIPS FOR SELLING MORE

1. People will not just buy from your website, so you must find other ways of pitching your products

2. You have to present the offer and ask them to buy

3. Improve conversion rates before you spend more money on putting more into the top of the funnel. This could be by improving your pitch

4. If you want to make FB richer, spend more to get more traffic going through your funnel, but if you want to get more sales, run more quarterly or monthly campaigns methodology that create rhythm in the business

5. Improve your presentation pack by getting some graphics work done. The more professional and well-presented your product, the more value that is placed upon it

6. Get some copywriting feedback

7. Learn some speaking skills

8. Develop a sales script

SUMMARY

The more recurring income, the larger your database and community, and the more your business valuation shoots up. If you have a recurring income in your business, then when you're valuing your business for exit, your valuation will be significantly higher, because that recurring income gives such a security to the business.

You can, of course, just sit back and enjoy it.

Aim to double your revenue in half the time. That is the outcome, because you've gone through this now – you've done Explore, you've done your Expressions of Interest, you've executed your product. You know how to do this. You've gone through the engagement piece. You've got your income sorted. You've then got money being generated that you can invest back into the course and seriously scale. Stand back and think strategically about what's next and what you want to do.

EXTEND
KEY LEARNINGS

1. Improve your conversions by 10%; this is the same as putting 50% more people in the top of the funnel.

2. Outsource and invest in some of the initial work you have done that can now be fine-tuned.

3. Improve your copywriting to improve conversion.

4. Improve your follow-up sequences to improve the number of people that buy from you.

5. Extend your mailing list.

6. Use your mailing list.

7. Develop more lead magnets to get people into your funnels.

8. Work out LTV and cost of customer acquisition; buy more customers if it works.

9. Use Facebook ads and other PPC mechanisms to buy more customers into your funnels.

10. Use somebody else's funnel, either JV or use affiliates.

11. Put your prices up.

12. Sell more.

CHAPTER 16

THE 5 Es JOURNEY

"The journey of a thousand miles begins with one step."

LAO TZU

A REALISTIC STARTING POINT

£2000 – £5000 per month is where we want you to start, but most people can easily achieve that with 20 to 50 members at £100 per month. Remember, if you have a product that perhaps doesn't have an ROI, or it doesn't give people an investment back, then you might be looking at something like £40 to £50 a month and you're going to need 60 people on your membership to realise a similar level of income.

If you want to ratchet that up, then you want to look at doing £50 memberships and then trying to get 1,000 members on board. Memberships and online courses work really well for people who have some experience in business. A business that has email lists and existing customers can get those first 20 to 30 customers on board fairly easily and get started and get moving.

STAGE 1 – PLAN YOUR GOALS

I want you to go ahead and plan how many members you hope to get, what targets you would need to hit, and where you think your pricing on your product will be each month. Write that down and start planning how many people you need and then check how many people you have on your business email list or how many existing customers you have in your database. Work out what percentage of those people you would need to convert to hit your first month target.

STAGE 2 – £2K-5K MONTHS

I can't wait for you to get to £2,000 – £5,000 a month. That's the next stage. We're looking for you to get to that magical number of £5,000 a month. For most people, that is a really magical number because it embodies everything that is high gross income and high fun. It is about having a relaxed lifestyle and having an income that supports your overhead costs and more! It normally covers the family, the holiday, the expenses of having a nice Christmas. It's all those great niceties in life that provide for you and your family. It's a really nice place to be.

The other thing that £5,000 a month gives you is some space to invest back into your membership and scale up. Scaling up will need you to perfect what works well for your customer demographic. You will need some investment capital to identify, test and measure new marketing funnels, copywriting,

66

You'll never want to go back to the lower numbers, because having a £10,000 a month programme is life changing.

99

graphic designs, new ad creatives, etc. Think about what you need to invest and where to bump up to the next stage.

STAGE 3 – £5K-10K MONTHS

The next stage of income is £5,000 – £10,000. The aim of our programme is to get you to £10,000 per month. To get you to that five figures, and investing back in your course and increasing your use of Facebook ads, PPC, SEO and Google ads, you need to be earning some income that can be invested back in. If you want to ramp up your success, get more traffic in at the top of the funnel and get people onto your list. Then move these people through your customer journey, give them content, free information, free white papers and free gifts that get them to become big fans of your product and buy.

You need them to trust you. Once you get to £10,000 per month that will give you huge satisfaction.

You'll never want to go back to the lower numbers, because having a £10,000 a month programme is life changing.

It is a product that you can run from anywhere in the world and it enables you to travel anywhere in the world. It gives you that freedom of income you've been looking for. Once you've got £10,000 a month coming in, a lot of people would have to cancel overnight for you to lose all that income. It becomes a very secure method of working, and I think it creates a stable state of psychological happiness and security because you

THE 5 ES JOURNEY

have that secure freedom that enables you to relax, but also enjoy the process of running this IP business.

STAGE 4 – £10K–100K MONTHS

The next stage is getting from £10,000 to £100,000. Not everybody can do that, and it can take a lot of work to do this. To go from £10,000 to £100,000 you're going to have to 10x it, as Grant Cardone would say, which really makes you think differently.

How could you drive 10 times the amount of people to your programme every month? How could you drive 10 times the conversions every month? How could you stop 10 times the churn? What other programmes could you align with? Who could you affiliate with? Where could you earn income from that would serve your members and your audience?

CHAPTER 17

CONCLUSION

"Give a man a fish, feed him for a day. Teach a man to fish, feed him for life."

CHINESE PROVERB

Just 26 of the super-rich people have the same amount of money as half of the world, says Oxfam's annual wealth report. Oxfam says that people are dying and being denied an education because of the way wealth is distributed.

My reason to help others is to help educate more people in creating wealth and the life they dream of, and with that financial and time freedom, enable them to contribute to the challenges of educating the world's poorest. I cannot change the world on my own, I can only make a small ripple of change. I hope that this ripple will spread out and we can create online courses to help educate the world's poorest adults and children with an E-Learning course.

So why do I want you to achieve this? It is really important to me that more people have more fun. Life is a gift and each second is something I believe we should all appreciate. Having money is not greedy or the route of all evil if you can use it to help others and your family.

Money significantly helps families to enjoy time together, to have family holidays and to enjoy the many wonders of the world. I strongly believe that if you have a gift, some experience or a unique way of thinking, then this alone is your life's purpose to share. Then, if that knowledge can bring more fun, more understanding and more money into the world then I too have achieved my life's purpose. You can have more money and more fun.

I know how hard you are working and understand that it's stressful and overwhelming. It is a strain to run a small business. There is always a challenge, from clients not paying invoices to staff calling in sick to increased international competition. This method could transform your life with more money and more fun. I hear your pain. I've been there and had those months where I have worked all hours only to find out there was nothing left for me once the VAT man had been paid. Now I have much more fun and money, I can choose to invest in the business, I can invest in my learning, I have time to write books and empower others. I can help those in poverty and provide families with a decade of clean drinking water. I go on holidays and re-energise. I recently went to Belgium and bought a kilo of the finest Belgian chocolates and, as a family, we gorged on them in one day. They were so amazing. It was the best memory for me and my kids. My daughter still complains she didn't get her fair share, which is a cute memory for her to have. I've promised her we will go back and get some more one day. I expect we will go again. I'm not worried about the cost of taking my family on a chocolate holiday. I don't worry about the money coming in and I have plenty of fun. I want to free you from the shackles of running your business and inject some fun back into your life.

There is also a huge amount of satisfaction in teaching and educating someone else to do well. It makes you dig deep, to get your methodology and structure spot on. It makes you raise your game. Teaching others, as you will do, also has massive benefits to your business. It's a double whammy; you teach and you learn more.

MY EXPERIENCE, YOUR BENEFIT

I'm delighted to share with you a method that has taken many years of perfecting and making mistakes. I am sure there are plenty of ways to make lots of money in online courses, but this process has worked for me and other course writers I have introduced this method to.

I wrote a substantial amount of this book whilst on a family holiday and cruise, sat on the balcony watching the sea. Wi-Fi is pretty poor on a cruise ship, but, in fact, because the online courses we run are so self-sufficient there hasn't been any need to panic about staying in touch on the laptop. We've managed a few things from the little Wi-Fi we had in ports and everything else has been no hassle at all. It was great to check in with our programmes and see that our income was building in the Stripe account ready to hit the bank account. Money is earnt whilst we are sleeping.

There was a time when a holiday would cost twice as much as the holiday itself because of the lost revenue while we took time off, but with this product the revenue is still coming in. We owned and ran a pub once and taking a week off cost us thousands of pounds as we had to employ someone to keep our business open while we were on holiday. That's not fun.

The key attribute we were looking for in online courses was the reliable monthly income. It was the ability to earn and rely on the income being generated because there is a strong asset backing everything up.

If you are planning on getting wealthy and living a life of comfort, travel and health without worrying about money, then I urge you to find assets that provide recurring incomes. Lumpy cash windfalls and big paydays are nice but only when you have the housekeeping money sorted. It's no fun to wait for big paydays, typically the timing is always longer, and the costs go up and your return on investment drops.

I love the cleverness of the online digital world and now that digital has taken the risk out of marketing, there is a way to scale. Test and measure small and then go big.

I have enjoyed writing this process out and developing the methodology. I hope that you can make lots of money with it.

My aim is to get you to five-figure months. I want you to do this to get to a place where you can scale and keep doubling your income. I am convinced some mentees' products can earn £83,334 or eighty-eight thousand and three hundred and four pounds per month (I'll let you do the maths). Is that your knowledge and your course?

THE 3 THINGS YOU NEED TO MAKE YOUR ONLINE COURSE A SUCCESS

Please invest in getting these 3 things right. If you cut any one out you will short change your results. You will fail with only 1 pillar in place and you can get some average results with 2 out of 3 pillars, but with all 3 pillars you will get exceptional results. It's worth putting the effort into the pillars, none are particularly complicated and they are fairly simple to achieve too. To summarise the 3 pillars:

1. You know what your IP is and it's got to be worth something to someone else.

    Whatever IP is and isn't, it is something of value that someone else is wanting to learn from you. IP can be anything. It's a hobby, course, flower arranging, coffee making, it's educating others in etiquette, it could be historic royal tales or painting cow pictures. But you have to have a depth of knowledge, experience and ideas to give your subscribers value.

2. You need to create content and a structure of deliverables that forms the basis of a really good subscription.

    Structure helps us all consume and enjoy the world. Using your content and aligning it with a time line will secure your income. It is the anchor on which your content and, therefore, income relies.

3. You must sell it.

Whatever you create, you need to sell. You know you can't stick it on your website and send one email out. You know that. You just need me to remind you of what you know. You don't need to be busy selling 24-7. I understand the resistance to sell but you are selling online, and you have to shout online about what you do. You can't build up the word of mouth in quite the same way. Your local market is quite small, and you are reaching out to a global market. To get heard across the other side of the world you will need to sell. Selling is fun anyway, once you realise the lifetime value and average subscriber revenues, you instantly see the money rolling in from the number of subscribers that join you.

THE HOW TO: THE 5 ES OF E-LEARNING

The way I help people is I've developed a process for helping them take their idea or material online, it's the 5 Es:

▶ **EXPLORE**

We start with the problem "I don't know what my IP is." We take you from "I have an idea" to Expressions of Interest.

▶ **EXPRESSIONS OF INTEREST**

We start with the problem "Is my IP worth something?" The test of success is "can you pre-sell your idea and get people on board?"

▶ **EXECUTE**

We start with the problem "I don't know how to write and produce my course?" The outcome is that we will write our first content and release it to our new members.

▶ ENGAGE

We start with the problem "How do I get to five-figure months?" We solve this by testing and measuring and growing through proven strategies. We improve the product and engage more customers for longer.

▶ EXTEND

We start with the problem "What do I stop doing and what am I doing well? I don't want to break good, but some bits need tweaking." We solve this by identifying leveraging, outsourcing and partnering in the course to reach six-figure months.

You will help your subscribers through your product value chain and all the knowledge and wisdom you have. Your ecosystem will evolve. I can help you do all of the above. I can do it for you but not without you. Invest in yourself and monetise your knowledge. Your knowledge has a purpose and a value to others. Help other people to help yourself. Give away your life's learning and you will get back so much and be handsomely rewarded.

If you achieve any recurring revenues per month, I want to know. Message or email me at Lorraine@lorrainegannon.com I will help everyone that reaches out to me. Find me on Facebook or LinkedIn, send me a screenshot of your income. If you want some help starting, fill out the idea & asset audit spreadsheet, there are some practical tips based on your score.

WWW.LORRAINEGANNON.COM/MOREMONEYMOREFUN

Time, freedom and fun are derivatives of money. Helping more people is a benefit of having more money. I want to help millions of girls and boys who live in third world countries to go to school and get an education and not have to walk miles for water every day. I want those girls and boys to start small businesses and borrow money to buy stock and sell that stock at a profit. Those girls and boys will invest in their communities and children and they will thrive and beat poverty. I can't do any of these things without time and financial freedom.

CHAPTER 18

HOW TO SET YOURSELF UP FOR SUCCESS

"If you can't fly then run, if you can't run then walk, if you can't walk then crawl, but whatever you do you have to keep moving forward."

MARTIN LUTHER KING, JR.

YOUR MINDSET

Some people will follow this exact process as laid out in the book and achieve great things and some of you won't follow the process and still achieve great results. Nothing matters more than your ability to try, and just take some action. If you believe you can then you will, and if you believe you can't do it then you have already failed. I believe that procrastination is a result of being overwhelmed and it comes from the lack of order and planning in your life and business and where you place you focus. To achieve the results you want, you need to plan what you are going to do.

YOUR COMMUNITY/TRIBE

The state of your mind and beliefs is so important to your success. You should surround yourself with successful people and go online and hang out with likeminded people on a community board like Facebook groups or LinkedIn groups. Seeing that other people have achieved results will significantly help you to achieve a good, positive mindset.

AVOID OVERWHELM

If you think too far ahead in any process you are bound to come up with an area that challenges you and that can lead you to predict a false failure too soon. Challenges will always bring up a sense of inadequacy and not knowing enough. Try to take one step at a time, and only work out what you need to do next. Plan what you need to do for each step.

Right at the beginning of this book we talked about how community and the evolution of our species has relied on wisdom and knowledge being passed down and taught from elders to the younger members. Trust yourself to find others that can help you achieve your goal too.

"Every minute you spend in planning saves 10 minutes in execution; this gives you a 1000% Return on Energy."

BRIAN TRACY

If you want to do this, do it. Take one step forwards each and every day until you are achieving your goals.

Use resources

Try and find resources and situations that help you. If you need to spend 2-3 days recording and producing content, book it out in your diary and get it done. Fixing short term and urgent jobs will not move you forwards. You need to put a period of work into getting the job done. Perhaps look to move out of your normal environment and book into a meeting room or other quiet place and spend some concentrated time working on this project.

"If you want to change your life, begin by changing your words. Start speaking the words of your dreams, of who you want to become, not the words of fear or failure."

ROBERT KIYOSAKI

AND FINALLY

Are you a little bit daunted and perhaps a bit scared of moving forwards? There is no need to be, I've given you plenty of tools to help you overcome procrastination and methodologies to help you break each stage into bite-sized chunks. I understand how you feel but unless you move forwards you will always be standing still here. If here is not where you want to be, you will need to move in a direction, it doesn't really matter which direction you go.

The 5 Es Methodology has been developed for the time pressured entrepreneur. You need feedback straight away that your online course is not working or a way to quantify how big a success it will be, so you can prioritise. But let none of this stop you from trying and starting. I have kept this process deliberately light. I have only asked you to think of your subject and then to develop an outline that you will put on a landing page; you write one webinar to sell it and a few emails to advertise your webinar. Then you just have to see what results you get in. The first time this process was run in our business we had 14 people on the webinar and one sale. Then it was just repetition. Now we take over 520 people through our courses each year.

You might be a bit scared to get out of your comfort zone. Don't cheat yourself out of this opportunity. There is a huge market in E-Learning. You can play small and be scared by what your friends and family might say, because they're the people you are worried about, right? It's not your clients and it's not your boss. I've just given you a way to sack your boss and leave your job. I've given you a way to fire your clients, perhaps some or maybe all of them. It's up to you. The only person holding you back is you and your beliefs. Your beliefs determine your behaviour. If you don't believe you can do this then you will find an excuse to avoid doing it.

Create the actions that are needed to make your online course a success. Choose to believe empowering thoughts and create opportunities. Choose what to focus on, then your results and success will come much quicker. Realise your value, stand behind your experience and leverage your results.

The real question is "when will you do this?"

It's about changing lives.

Start with yours.

CAN I HELP YOU?

BOOK A STRATEGY CALL WITH ME

WWW.LORRAINEGANNON.COM/MOREMONEYMOREFUN

(ENDNOTES)

1 Ebbinghaus Forgetting curve

2 https://www.onlineeducation.com/guide/online-learning-faqs

3 Onlineedcuation.com

4 http://reports.weforum.org/future-of-jobs-2016/skills-stability/#view/fn-13

5 http://reports.weforum.org/future-of-jobs-2016/skills-stability/#view/fn-13

6 https://www.forbes.com/sites/tjmccue/2018/07/31/e-learning-climbing-to-325-billion-by-2025-uf-canvas-absorb-schoology-moodle/#522094e13b39

7 https://merchdope.com/youtube-stats/

8 https://blog.hootsuite.com/youtube-stats-marketers

9 https://moz.com/beginners-guide-to-seo/how-people-interact-with-search-engines

10 https://www.slideshare.net/Micro-Focus/growth-of-internet-data-2017

11 https://www.slideshare.net/Micro-Focus/growth-of-internet-data-2017

12 https://readwrite.com/2012/02/29/interview_changing_engines_mid-flight_qa_with_goog/

13 https://blog.microfocus.com/how-much-data-is-created-on-the-internet-each-day/

14 https://www.statista.com/statistics/273018/number-of-internet-users-worldwide/

15 https://blog.microfocus.com/how-much-data-is-created-on-the-internet-each-day/

16 MarketingSherpa

17 InsideSales.com

18 https://www.mckinsey.com/business-functions/marketing-and-sales/our-insights/why-marketers-should-keep-sending-you-emails

19 https://blog.boomerangapp.com/2017/05/the-one-thing-you-should-never-do-in-an-email-subject-based-on-data/

20 https://www.experian.co.uk/assets/marketing-services/white-papers/wp-personalisation-retail-marketing.pdf

21 https://www.campaignmonitor.com/resources/guides/email-marketing-new-rules/

Lightning Source UK Ltd.
Milton Keynes UK
UKHW010652011119
352680UK00002B/218/P

9 781913 036379